IT WOOD BE FUN
Woodworking with Children

Michael Bentinck-Smith

illustrations designed by

Michael Bentinck-Smith

and rendered by Derek Aylward

Published by Martin and Lawrence Press
Groton, Massachusetts

Designed by Sally Reed, The Quick Brown Fox, Groton, MA

Published by:
Martin and Lawrence Press
PO Box 682
Groton, MA 01450

PRINTED IN CANADA

ISBN 978-0-9820732-0-9

Words to Live and Grow By

■ How are you going to be a success without doing the work?
When did you decide you couldn't do it? Yesterday? Five minutes ago?
■ Look at that! See what happens when that good brain of yours goes to work? Things get done and problems get solved.
■ Quitters never win; winners never quit.
■ I know you are terrific but nobody else will know if you don't set your sights higher and do your best. You need to act terrific.
■ You have a chance to be outstanding and you are going to settle for ordinary and average?
■ Is this your best effort? If it is, I bet I will love it too.
■ Professionals judge their own work.
■ Professionals don't like holidays on their projects. Professionals hate rubber nails.
■ You already know! Have faith in your decision, you did the work.
■ Good stuff doesn't come easily, it takes hard work. That's why everyone wants the good stuff.
■ Don't forget to give yourself a pat on the back - you did it.
■ We always go for the "terrific" and the "wonderful" here.
■ We have fun accomplishing things, enjoying our successes. We aren't wasting time with bad behavior.
■ Love what you do. You will have fun and be successful.
■ The harder you work, the better it gets.
■ I'm here to help you, not to do your work — you have to take the first step.
■ There is nothing you can do to this project by accident that we can't fix together.
■ Is it silky smooth and terrific? Is it holiday free? Then it is finished.
■ Ever try to put on your underwear after you put on your pants? It is important to remember to complete one step before jumping to the next.
■ I'm not sure how to help you. Guess you didn't like any of my ideas as I notice you didn't bother with my directions.
■ This is not my first rodeo. I have done this before and that way won't work, but if you really want to try, see what happens. Maybe you will get lucky.

- Sometimes we make our own luck.
- Sometimes mistakes teach us a lot. We can figure out what went wrong.
- We are really successful only when we complete the things we start.
- The best ideas in the world don't amount to much if they don't turn into something.
- Do you know what happens to a parakeet when you shoot it with an elephant gun? Be gentle and thoughtful with your work.
- That's the price of fame. People copy us when we have great ideas and do great things.
- Good projects take time. Rush it and you will probably blow it.
- I never said this would be easy. I did say it could be done.
- We have to be serious about the choices we make — there are some that can't be easily thrown in the wastebasket if they don't work out.
- You are a success because you think ahead, make plans and decisions about your future. Those good ideas will get you somewhere. Good for you!
- Razzle-dazzle and whiz-bang is easy and just a cover up for the real deal. Anyone can be fast, not everyone can be good. Good takes work.
- Being first in line doesn't mean much. The better we are, pretty soon winning and being first will take care of itself.
- Experts use the right tool for the right job.
- We have to learn to take care of ourselves and our things – that's not someone else's job.
- Things don't always come out perfect; don't worry; just keep working toward your goals.
- Can't ever be a winner without playing the game.

— M. B.-S.

Acknowledgements

I wish to express my gratitude to the many people who influenced, inspired, and supported the writing of this book. Among those particularly generous and thoughtful: Melinda D'Arbeloff comes to mind for providing the original inspiration and much help in the manuscript's early organization and editing; Lynda Johnson and Simmons College for organization, typing, and encouragement; Helen Haynes and William and Elizabeth Atwood, who introduced me to various publishing options; Sally Reed for book design and production, the Doctors Samaraweera whose knowledge of children, general good sense, and long-standing friendship often covered my own rough spots in life as well as in the book; my friend A. Robert Phillips who always encouraged and often pushed me through the process, and last but far from least, all the wonderful children, parents, and coworkers who made it all happen.

I wrote this book in grateful acknowledgement of my strong willed and supportive parents Phebe and William Bentinck-Smith, and to the loving amazement of my sisters Judy Covin and Nancy Soulette, and my brother Peter Bentinck-Smith. Thanks also to my son Andy Bentinck-Smith, who has enriched my future with two wonderful grandsons, Ethan and Evan. Aunt Joan and Cousin Charlotte, this one is for you! Thanks

—M.B.S.

Dedication

This book is dedicated to all children. They are the future.
Each one deserves validation, support, love,
and an equal opportunity to thrive and succeed.
We adults need to ensure this, and enjoy
the wonderful progression of childhood.
We can all make this world a better place,
and our small people are a crucial part.
They depend on us, our guidance and support.

—M. B.-S.

IT WOOD BE FUN
Woodworking with Children

INTRODUCTION

"Put the kids in charge"

I am Michael Bentinck-Smith, the woodworking teacher at the Lower School of Milton Academy, in Milton, Massachusetts, where for 41 years, between 1966 and 2007, I taught kindergarten through sixth grade. When I began, I had little idea how fulfilling and enjoyable the job would be. There were few days I came to work without a smile, uplifted by the knowledge I would learn something new, and have a great day — a big blessing, to say the least.

Over the years, I have been asked from time to time why I have not written a book. I never took the idea seriously until recently, when I realized the woodwork classes had evolved into a truly productive experience with enduring qualities for the children. Writing this book has given me the happy opportunity to pass along some of what I have learned.

This book is geared for five through ten-year-olds — ages when much can be done to tap into a child's imagination, willingness to learn, and eagerness to try new things. Successful projects come from imagination and commitment, as well as courage, hard work, self-respect, and belief a project can be done. From a sense of competence comes self-confidence. It's a circular process based on positive experiences with tools and wood. I know this works. I have watched kids carry their projects home like the Holy Grail, with love and pride. The tangible object is the fun part for them; they have earned their reward and they know it. But we know what they get out of the process lasts forever.

Former students so often tell me how they still have their cherished project — a mailbox, a birdhouse, a castle, or a table, and how much it still means to them. (The survival rate for these projects is quite remarkable!) I have seen so many amazing results over the years. I am hoping this book can perpetuate such good energy and realize the wonderful potential of five- to ten-year-old children.

Simple and straightforward

Hand skills — the ability to make and fix things — can be empowering. It Wood be Fun attempts to share the knowledge and pleasure that comes through learning to use hand tools to make objects of increasing complexity and challenge. It leads parents and teachers through the first steps of equipping a toolbox and buying (or finding) materials to set up a workshop (small, simple, and temporary works as well as spacious and permanent), and a child-sized workbench. From there it's a single step into the world of woodworking, beginning with ultra simple and creative fantasy projects and moving on through the dozen projects in this book arranged in order of gradually increasing difficulty that will encourage your child to develop skill, confidence, and know-how.

It Wood be Fun begins with a list of recommended tools and materials followed by brief but thorough discussions of their care, storage, and proper handling, and a few words on recommended wood and where to get it. Before moving into the project section, I take up practical matters of safety, dealing with anger or frustration, bruised thumbs, estimating timing, and other challenges inherent in working with kids. Now comes the simplest (and maybe most satisfying) projects of all, those that come directly from your young child's imagination – the fantasy projects that may range from sanding a block of wood to nailing two pieces of wood together to make a boat, space station, or airplane. Simple, satisfying, fun to play with, fantasy projects are perfect for getting your five- or six-year-old child acquainted with handling wood and tools. A series of further practical lessons and demonstrations follow. These will introduce you and your child to tricks of the trade — tips on measuring, pattern-making, and assembly.

With respect to safety, by the way, be reassured that woodworking with hand tools presents little if any danger to children, so long as the tools are well-cared for and properly used. (Even a Popsicle stick can prove hazardous in the wrong hands!) This section is filled with sensible precautions and instructions for such safe
handling.

The fun begins with the projects. Geared for young children, designed, tested, and proved by their peers — this collection of more than a dozen woodworking projects will teach you and your child a lot about woodworking. If the subject sticks, as it did with me, there is no limit to where your child might take his or her newfound skills and sense of accomplishment. In the meantime, the learning and fun involved in the process is really all that matters.

No project is complete without paint and other finishes. Seeing a robot or car come alive with a coat of paint brings so much delight. At the end of the projects section, I offer general information which will provide you with all you need to know to bring a project to completion.

It Wood be Fun resembles a toolbox for parents. It contains all the information you need to work successfully with young children, including supportive advice culled from years of experience. The most important thing I have to impart is respect — respect for children, respect for tools, and respect for a hands-on experience that will bring pleasure, self-confidence, and real competence to anyone who gets involved. Like juggling and other hand-eye coordination skills, learning to use tools, to measure carefully, to cut accurately, to smooth thoroughly, and to bring a woodworking project to completion can have implications for a child's well-being, concentration, self-confidence, work ethic and patience that will affect all other areas of life, including classroom learning. Not to mention the sheer joy involved in working together— parent and child.

My approach to working with children

Each child is an individual — valuable and important. By engaging with children on a woodworking project in which they can take responsibility, ownership, and pride, you are saying to children: "Put it out there, go for the whole enchilada, be a winner, you can do it. This time is about you!"

What does this really mean? In my classroom, it meant I put the kids in charge. They made choices and took responsibility for their own work. With a little planning and preparation, you can do this, too. Kids do come up with ideas and you can help turn those ideas into reality. You can sneak in the "education" part as and when needed. You can have fun but instill a serious and committed attitude toward work. Very early on, you can make it plain quitting was not an option.

Let me introduce you to my classroom: On the first day of kindergarten, I show the children the woodwork room, the tools, the work area, and wood supply. Then I introduce myself and say, "I am your teacher and this is your class." Then I stand back to see what happens. In this moment of quiet, the kids give each other incredulous looks — they are not used to having such freedom in the classroom! Before long a courageous one will go after a tool or a piece of wood and want to do something with it. I'm ready to help and give advice. Within five minutes, they are all off and running. The rest is history. In those first five minutes two crucial things have happened: Each child has started to direct him or herself and each has made a choice (if not two or three).

How much autonomy do five-year-olds have in their lives? Not much. When they discover that in my classes they are autonomous and they call the shots, the sense of freedom is electrifying. Of course, I guide their choices so their experiences have the potential for success.

Similarly, if you give children a sense of responsibility and trust —their job is to act accordingly. They make a bad choice, they own it; they make a mess they own that too; they work hard and pull through, they have earned a rich sense of accomplishment. Held accountable, they soon realize the road to success is within their grasp. Failure has no place, nor is anyone else to blame for mistakes or mishaps.

Parents as teachers

So far I have had a lot to say about the child's part of the process. Adults are hugely important, of course! Parents and other teachers are especially vital to a child's first successful experience of woodworking. Our children respect and love us, often without reservation. This is a golden opportunity to share a truly fun and productive experience. It is unlikely a child will venture into the material and projects in this book if their parents are not "on the same page." Take advantage of the many "teachable moments" that follow as your child progresses through this process.

Do be wary of picking a project that appeals to you, however, and creating a situation of unrealistic expectation or unfulfilled dreams. Let's keep the kids in charge. That which piques the imagination and fires the enthusiasm of a child will almost always be a success. All we really have to do is prime the pump, encourage, guide, and support. The kids do the rest. I hope this book will give you the emotional and physical tools and skills you need to have a wonderful time teaching your child to make woodworking projects. A successful project is a great triumph for a child. The thrill can be life-long.

A word about tools

No attempt is made to include power tools in this book. My feeling is that power tools do not improve ability, just speed. Kids make a bigger mess faster with a power tool and the chances of an accident are greatly increased. Hand tools mandate one-hundred percent participation, and that's what any good woodworking class or project with children is all about. Nothing happens before the hand skills are learned.

Looking ahead: what's next?

Let's say woodworking catches on, and over a few years you and your child have completed the projects in this book. By then, your child will have learned a series of invaluable basic woodworking skills. Indeed, there is no end to the uses and projects to which good carpentry skills can be put, and no end to the satisfaction to be gained from beautiful workmanship. This book ends with a few words of advice and suggestions for the woodworker who wants to continue.

> "Good stuff doesn't come easily, it takes hard work. That's why everyone wants the good stuff."

Or, let's say your child enjoys woodworking but moves on to other things — physics or ice hockey or writing. That's fine, too.

The pleasure and confidence gained from engaging in these projects will continue to prove itself throughout a lifetime.

CREATE A WORK AND STORAGE AREA

Getting started

Looking after woodworking tools empowers young woodworkers and teaches them important lessons for future success. Learning to use their tools correctly and for the right purpose puts kids in control. The care, storage, organization, and maintenance of tools are all part of the craft of woodworking. We generally do better work

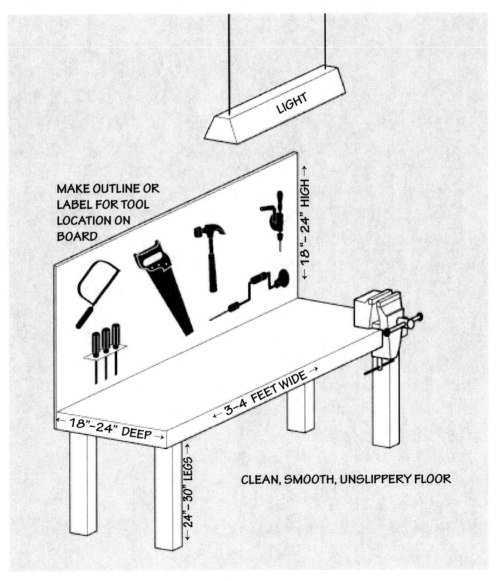

LIGHT

MAKE OUTLINE OR LABEL FOR TOOL LOCATION ON BOARD

← 18"–24" HIGH →

← 3–4 FEET WIDE →

← 18"–24" DEEP →

← 24"–30" LEGS →

CLEAN, SMOOTH, UNSLIPPERY FLOOR

when our equipment is in good condition, and our work area is neat and arranged with efficiency in mind.

There are two approaches to keeping tools organized and within easy reach: a toolbox or container where tools can "live" when not in use; or a storage board on a wall close to the work area where tools can hang. On a board, each tool's location can be marked, outlined, or labeled. Tools hanging on a board are visible and readily accessible when the time comes to go back to work. A missing tool is instantly noticed – this helps children realize they haven't put something away and will come up short when they need it again. Reaching for a hanging tool is somewhat easier than digging through a toolbox. For these reasons, a tool board generally works best when there is room. Boxes are compact, however, more mobile when space is an issue, and perfectly doable. After all, what's more classic than the carpenter with his toolbox?

Now, let's consider the work area — essentially a child-sized workbench with all tools within a child's reach. A workbench is best when it is solid, stable, and made to have a vise attached to it. It needs to be a good height for children, 24 to 30 inches high generally works well but you will want to measure to fit your child. Pre-made workbenches can be expensive, especially if bought new, and they take up room. In seeking alternatives or something that can be disassembled when not in use, an area as small as three-feet by two-feet can do the job — thus an old, heavy table or desk, a cabinet or low bureau, even a flat door on boxes or stands attached to a wall with "L" brackets will suffice. (I do advise against using kitchen counters or dining room tables because work areas can and will become battle scarred.)

Just remember, the more solid the work area the better. Woodworkers need to saw, block plane, carve, or chisel without a tip-over. With so many new things to learn, you will want to reduce the external frustrations as much as possible.

Having a place to work, as well as to keep tools establishes boundaries. Children will know where they can perform their magic. The more available the space, the closer one can get to the ideal setting of a well-defined and accessible tool board or box, and a large, solid, and anchored work area. It goes without saying that reasonable lighting and smooth, safe flooring make all the difference. Rough or slippery floors and poor visibility add nothing to the good time.

Things to consider:

1. Overall height and depth: Children need to be able to reach the tools with comfort. (By the way, do take left-handed children into consideration by allowing them to choose — for example, putting the vise on the left side of the bench.)

2. The arrangement of tools on the storage board or in the tool box is arbitrary, although I do give some guidelines when discussing individual tools in the following chapters. It is good to involve children in the decision making; letting them make choices promotes a sense of enthusiasm and ownership. When all is arranged to satisfaction, you can designate permanent locations for everything, subject to change if experience suggests a better idea.

"Look at that! See what happens when that good brain of yours goes to work? Things get done and problems get solved."

BUILDING A TOOLBOX FOR LIFE

Tools make it all happen. My maternal grandfather died twenty years before I was born, but his tools were (with some exceptions, of course) available to me as a child. As no one else in my family took an interest in woodworking, I experimented with my grandfather's tools on my own, making mess after mess before managing to teach myself real woodworking skills. So began a lifelong interest and affection for tools and putting them to creative use.

The tools needed for the work outlined in this book are bare bones basic and relatively inexpensive. Just make sure you choose tools of good quality. Cheap or "toy" tools are no bargain. They often break, can cause hurt to someone or something, and do not do the job. For children, this can turn woodworking into an exercise in frustration (in which they will quickly lose interest). Remember, too, children may end up keeping these first tools their whole lives. You don't grow out of a screw driver, for example. I know adults who still use the tools they acquired as children or adolescents.

You will want to keep tools well-maintained for safety and easy use. Sharp cutting tools, a hammer head tightly secured to its handle, clean screwdrivers, and whole saw blades make for an enticing and practical setup. Badly kept tools defeat the purpose; good quality, well-functioning tools enhance the experience.

Where do we get good tools? Name brands show up at hardware stores big and small, although the prices may be better at the larger stores. It is important to pick at least the middle grade of each item. Be wary of package deals! They don't always include all the needed tools and the quality can be unreliable. In general, the more one spends, the better and safer the tool.

Going for new is the fastest way out. A slower but much cheaper route involves buying used tools at consignment and thrift shops, flea markets, and yard sales. Just do watch for cheap, defective, or inoperable tools. The stakes aren't very high in the used arena, however, so in the worst-case scenario a tool may end up in the wastebasket, and you may have to go on another shopping trip.

Kids take delight in tool-gathering expeditions. Flea markets and yard sales are like big treasure hunts to them. When you find great tools in odd or out-of-the-way places after a search that adds to their value, somehow. Those tools found in the trash or in a special deal of some kind over the years have particular meaning to me. My tool collection is life-long and a work in progress but it started here — with the basics.

TOOLS

Hammer

Crosscut saw

Coping saw

Chisel(s)

Hand (eggbeater) drill

Drill bit(s)

Block plane

Oilstone

Screwdriver assortment

Try square

Ruler

Carving "sloyd" knife

4-way (or assorted) wood rasps

C-clamps 4"- 6" (2)

Vise for workbench

MATERIALS

Wood glue

16" lengths 1x8 #2 pine

1 1/2", 2" finish nails

1 1/2" butt hinges and screws

Wood, carpet, wallpaper, and cloth scraps

This is the start of a wonderful adventure! More information about each item on the list follows.

Shopping List

TOOLS

- **Block plane** — Stanley or comparable quality — knob to adjust blade (also called an iron)

- **12 oz. claw hammer** — Stanley or comparable quality

- **8" try square** (or combination square) Stanley or comparable

- **4-way combination rasp** (Vermont American or comparable quality)

- **6 1/2" pin type coping saw** — Stanley or comparable (2 blades per package) – Great Neck seem to work well

- **24-30" crosscut hand saw** (or "toolbox saw") Stanley or comparable

- **Screwdriver assortment** — Phillips and regular – Stanley Handyman work well or comparable

- **Hand or "eggbeater" drill** – Stanley or comparable

- **3/8, 1/4, 1/8 drill bits or set** — don't have to be wonderful —, for wood only will do.

- **Bit brace** – Stanley Handyman is fine

- **3/4 auger bit** (or set)
- **Chisels:** 3/8" at least or 1/4 and 1/2 (or set) — good ones survive hammering

- **Oilstone** — fine and coarse hator or Vermont grits — American or comparable

- **Two C-clamps** — Brink and Cotton or comparable

- **Staple gun**

- **4" Carving knife**

SUPPLIES AND MATERIALS

ESSENTIALS

5# box each 1 1/2", 2" finish nails

16-inch lengths of 1 x 8 #2 pine

3-inch steel hasps best for safes and trunks

Large squeeze bottle carpenters yellow glue

Best hinges, easiest to use: 1 1/2 inch butt steel hinges

Bottle kits (for making bottles into lamps) best for the lamp projects

Scrap soft wood: pine or basswood 1/2 inch thick for practice or project "accessories"

NICE ADDITIONS

(for the dollhouse, the birdhouse, and the car in particular)

Scrap dowels (round stock) 1/4, 3/8, bird house perches, boat mast, etc.

Scrap carpet — for dollhouse floors, cat and dog box lining, or stuffed animal nests (kids like bright colors when possible)

Scrap wallpaper — for houses, lining for boxes, etc.

Scrap rubber — car inner tubes are great — for drumheads, improvised hinges, etc.

Scrap rags or cloth – chair coverings or doll bedclothes, etc.

Scrap screen, rabbit or chinchilla wire, hardware cloth – great for cage doors, jails, etc.

A few words about wood

What is the best wood for projects with children? I recommend 16-inch lengths of 1 x 8 #2 pine (with some but not a ridiculous number of knots, likely mixed in with a few 16-inch 1 x 8 pieces of clear or knot-free pine). Number two pine makes a happy compromise. Clear or #1 pine is hideously expensive and hardly necessary.

The carving projects are best and easiest done with fairly clear stock. Knots not only create changes in the wood grain around them but are hard and difficult to carve; when chiseling little pieces can chip off as well, which creates an eye hazard! Carving frustration is minimized with clear stock.

Knots can be inconvenient when sawing and driving nails, but you can work around this. Help kids pick pieces in which the knots don't create a big interference (such as a big one right next to a saw cut or where a nail needs to be placed).

> "Is this your best effort? If it is, I bet I will love it too."

Pine is the wood of choice as it is soft, easily cut, planed, chiseled, or nailed. The cost is reasonable. Other soft woods could certainly be used, but they cost more.

One-by-eight-inch pine in 16-inch lengths sounds like an arbitrary measurement, but I have found it quite ideal for child-sized projects. Sixteen-inch pieces can easily be divided into two or four pieces. The modest length regulates the size of the project, preventing it from getting too big for a child to maneuver and causing loss of control, which can pave the way for frustration.

Hard woods are too difficult to work with; sawing and nailing is all but impossible for children, especially small ones. Plywood is not very satisfactory to work with, either, as cutting, shaping, and nailing without splitting the ends can prove difficult.

Very small children into fantasy projects really need soft wood. Frustration comes easily at this age and a taste of success early in the game creates the incentive to keep going.

Sources for lumber

The most obvious source for wood is a lumber yard or building supply store. In addition, one can often get soft wood scraps at a cabinet-making woodshop, or carpenter's workshop. Lumber can be cut to size at home, of course, but having the 1 x 8 cut into 16-inch lengths at the lumber yard or shop is the easiest if not the cheapest way to go. Pre-cut stock sets the appropriate limits and boundaries for the young woodworker, and avoids arguments about pieces being "too small."

Used wood also works, but do make sure it is soft, unfinished, and clean enough to use.

TOOLS: THEIR CARE AND USE

OILSTONE (Sharpening)

Cost: $12

Description: Oilstones are used for sharpening chisels, carving knives, and plane irons.

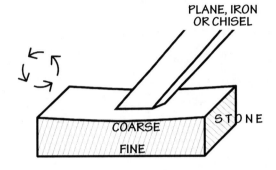

The most common are man-made rectangular blocks of carbarundum with coarse grit on one side, and fine on the other. The most useful size measures 2" x 6".

Technique: The proper technique for sharpening tools with an oilstone is easily learned.

Starting on the rough side (if the tool is very dull or chipped), work on the bevel first. Place the tool level on the stone and move gently in a circular motion all over the stone. During the honing, make sure the tool's angle remains the same. It should stay flat and square. When the edge gets sharp, do the same on the smoother side of the oilstone.

The final step is to lay the tool flat on its back and drag across the stone two or three times to get rid of the "hair" edge.

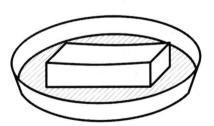

SOAK IN A SMALL PIE PLATE OR SIMILAR FOR ONE HOUR. FULLY SATURATE IN OIL.

New stones should be soaked in motor oil before use. SAE 30 is ideal oil but any engine oil will work. (Avoid other kinds of oil.) This lubricates the sharpening process. Soak for an hour or so, then drip dry on a paper towel before use.

Care: Oilstones are brittle; they break when dropped, so keep yours in a safe place such as its original box, or wrap in paper or rags. You will want to avoid dumping heavy tools on top of it in a tool-box. With proper care, an oilstone will last indefinitely.

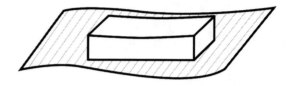

LAY ON A RAG OR PAPER TOWEL UNTIL "DRY." (WILL ALWAYS FEEL OILY!)

FOUR-WAY COMBINATION RASP

Cost: $8

Description and Function: A four-way combination rasp has a flat side and a rounded side, with fine and coarse teeth on each side. A good quality rasp will work well on wood for a long time.

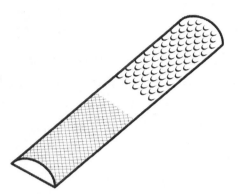

Use: The flat side is used for smoothing flat surfaces and outside corners; the curved side smoothes inside curves such as a castle door top, birdhouse hole, or doghouse door. Starting with the rough side for the mega bumps and finishing silky smooth with the fine will do a nice job.

Care: The rasp is designed for wood only; using it to smooth other materials such as plastic will quickly spoil it. Avoid throwing other tools on top of your rasp, and filing nail heads or the edge of a vise or clamp, which will damage the teeth. Always keep your rasp in an envelope or plastic bag.

Note: I don't mention sandpaper. Small children don't handle it well. It tears easily, they tend to waste it, and I have found that the 4 way combination rasp does a nice job for this purpose. Sandpaper is not cheap and it doesn't last well in small hands.

BLOCK PLANE

Cost: $35-$50

Description: A block plane is generally used for smoothing saw cuts, with and across the grain of a board. It can be used for sizing or shaping edges or sides of boards. Kids love using the block plane for rounding edges, planning mailbox roofs and sides of leg bases for tables or chairs. When planing with the grain, the curls of wood enrapture the user, as does the smooth result.

Block planes are pricey but a good one is worth the money. Cheap ones don't maintain their adjustment, dull quickly, and are generally frustrating to use. The plane need not have an adjustable throat (the opening where the wood chips come through) but it should have a knob at the rear for blade adjustment.

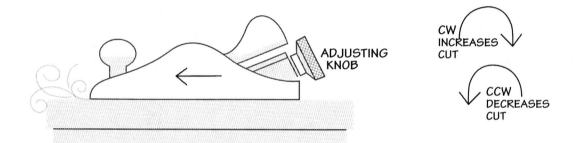

Technique: One large hand can often use a block plane but for children two small ones will always be needed. With the work piece in a vise, the planer should stand in back of the plane and push it across the wood. When planning with the grain, thin curls of wood will peel off. Remember to adjust the plane iron (blade) as needed. The plane should not rip off big strips, but likewise it should not fail to cut significantly. Experiment! Practice makes better.

PLANE STROKES

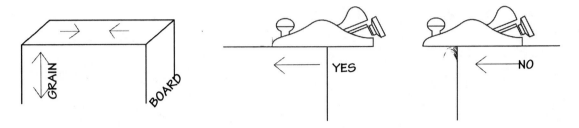

When planing across the grain, one needs to work from the edge toward the center of the work piece, or nasty chipping will result. Curls of wood don't appear in this instance, just powdery shavings. Careful adjustment helps productivity. When the blade is out too far, it hacks at the wood; when not far enough, it doesn't cut effectively.

Kids like experimenting. Practicing both skills on wood scraps is not a bad idea. It can prevent a child from brutalizing his or her project, while it entertains and teaches watchful patience and skill. I have had more than one child happily shave up a nice piece of wood just for the thrill of chips.

Care: Planes are cast iron. If they fall on a concrete floor, they will very likely break. Repairing is possible but difficult. Small hands often drop things. I keep a scrap of smooth carpet on the workplace floor to help prevent smashed planes and other mishaps.

Meanwhile, you will want to store the plane carefully as the plane iron can dull and chip easily if other metal tools bang into it. You can wrap a rag around it, or store separately. (Here's another instance where a tool board is preferable to a tool box.)

CHISEL

Cost: $10 each (sets can be bought at lower price per piece)

Description: Chisels are most often used for carving letters and shapes in wood. One-quarter-inch and 3/8-inch width chisels are most useful; wider are more difficult to manage. If your budget allows for only one chisel, a 3/8-inch will do nicely. Buy a good quality chisel; the cheaper ones don't stay sharp and the handles soon break.

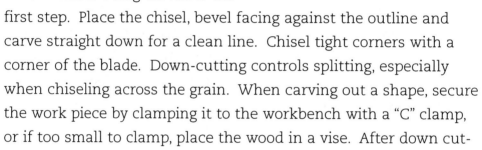

DOWN CUTTING A LETTER

Technique: Down cutting the perimeter of what is being carved is the first step. Place the chisel, bevel facing against the outline and carve straight down for a clean line. Chisel tight corners with a corner of the blade. Down-cutting controls splitting, especially when chiseling across the grain. When carving out a shape, secure the work piece by clamping it to the workbench with a "C" clamp, or if too small to clamp, place the wood in a vise. After down cut-ting is complete, carving begins. Keep the bevel side of the chisel face down to control the cut. (When carving with the bevel side up, the chisel will dig in like a shovel making a flat carve almost impossible.) Handle the chisel gently to carve out the desired shape, and when possible, carve with the grain. Marking a two-way arrow with the grain of wood helps young people remember which way to go. You will want to encourage your child to prac-tice on a wood scrap to get the feel of the chisel, the process, and the way the wood grain impacts the job.

BEVEL FACES WHAT IS BEING CARVED OUT

USE JUST THE CORNER OF THE CHISEL FOR A TIGHT CURVE OR CORNER

Care: Every tool that has a cutting edge is potentially hazardous and also susceptible to damage. I always encourage careful use of such tools. For storage, a chisel is best hung; taping or securing the blade protects it from chipping and dulling. If you store the chisel in a toolbox, it's good to tape the blade as well to prevent cutting oneself. Do remember, the chisel blades are cast steel and can snap off if used as a pry, or get ruined if used as a screwdriver.

COPING SAW

Cost: $5-10

Description: The 6 1/2 inch pin-type coping saw is the most popular variety. Blades are easy to change, and can be repositioned for cutting sideways by loosening the handle and rotating the blade. Although they cut fast, coping saw blades are easily broken.

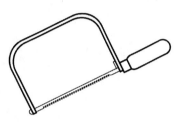

Use: Start the saw the same as a handsaw. You can decide how to position the blade so the cut is on the pull or the push stroke. Feeling the teeth on the blade will tell you which is preferable. The secret to success with a coping saw is to keep it straight.

Children seem to think they are going faster by angling the saw around a corner or racing through straight areas, pointing the saw up in the air. Not true. The cuts come out poorly, the project looks unnecessarily bumpy, and the blade is most likely to break when crookedly forced around corners. I encourage students to

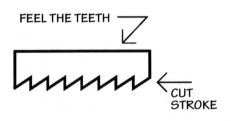

FEEL THE TEETH

CUT STROKE

practice using the coping saw. Success will bring satisfaction and good results.

Care: As with any saw, hanging is the best storage. The coping saw blades are quite fragile, and may get broken when buried under other tools in a box. Do use a coping saw with care: Cuts sustained

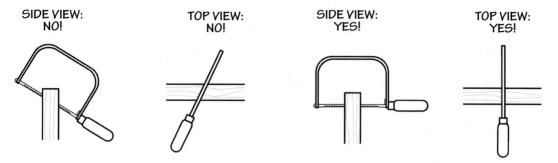

SIDE VIEW:
NO!

TOP VIEW:
NO!

SIDE VIEW:
YES!

TOP VIEW:
YES!

from careless handling are usually educational (the user learns new respect for the saw!) and far from life threatening. Meanwhile, the saw blades are designed for wood and will break quickly or get spoiled when used otherwise.

HANDSAW

Cost: $25-$40

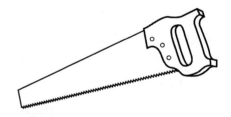

Description: Handsaws measuring 18- to 24-inches long are best for small children. Old-time conventional cut saws make the best choice as the teeth are "set (splayed out at the sides) so the kerf, or incision, is wide. This means the saw is less likely to stick in the wood while in use. Modern varieties have sharp, well designed teeth and work well, but must be kept sharp.

Use: The key to successful cutting is careful starting and cutting early in the game. Start the saw by sliding it backwards several times at the chosen spot until a small kerf (or groove) develops —to the point at which the saw will no longer jump out of the groove and cut in the wrong place when pushed forward. One hand holds the saw, the other guides it and keeps it steady.

When your child can easily push the saw forward (cutting

stroke), you will want to make sure she follows the cut line in the back stroke. Starting is easy at the beginning; it gets harder if the saw goes off course. If that

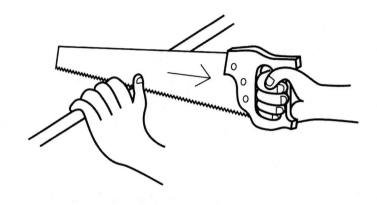

should happen (and undoubtedly will at some point!), just realign the saw where it started to veer off, twist in the right direction and re-cut.

Care: Woodworking saws are designed for wood only – no plastic, metals, or plaster. They will quickly spoil and dull if used otherwise. The safest way to store is by hanging on a board. Careful handling prevents damage to the saw and the user! Tool boxes make acceptable storage, too, but be careful when reaching for other tools in the box, as the blade can scratch your hand.

HAMMER

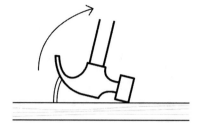

Cost: $8 – 15

Description: A 10- or 12-ounce standard claw hammer works best for basic woodworking. Lighter ones just don't have the heft need-ed to drive a nail and heavier ones are hard for small hands to man-age. A good hammer is money well-spent! (The claws won't break off when pulling nails, for example.)

Use: Starting a nail takes two hands. One hand places and holds the nail at its desired location and the other taps the nail hard enough to make it stand up on its own. The first hand now gets out of the way (less painful) and you can now start hammering the nail in the rest of the way. "Crooked starters are crooked enders," so the saying goes. The first few hard strokes are critical. Careful positioning of the nail minimizes "coming out parties" or "rubber nails." The trick is to keep the nail straight in the beginning so it can finish straight. If it starts straight, later bending can be straightened and the hammerer can keep going. Hammering is fun and excellent for developing eye-hand coordination. Encourage your child to practice.

You pull out a nail with the hammer claw. Hook the nail head in the claw, and pull with a rocking motion of the hammer while

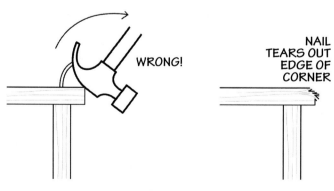

WRONG!

NAIL TEARS OUT EDGE OF CORNER

supporting the hammer on the surface of the wood through-out the process, otherwise the nail will tear itself through

the edge of the project and make a mess

RIGHT!

HAMMER IS SUPPORTED ON FLAT SURFACE OF WOOD. NAIL COMES OUT STRAIGHT.

Professionals don't like "rubber nails" or "coming out parties." You can encourage children to fix these problems. Protruding nails can usually be hammered out backwards and pulled from the top, bent over nails can usually be worked out with the claw but sometimes a screwdriver will dig the nail out further before you or your child hammer it out backwards and remove with the claw.

Care: You will want to help children realize tools are designed for a purpose and should be used that way. Claw hammers are meant only for woodworking, for example, and not for smashing rocks or anything else. Correctly used, a hammer is a safe and extremely handy tool. Hanging is ideal for storage, but a tool box also works nicely.

HAND "EGGBEATER" DRILL & DRILL BITS

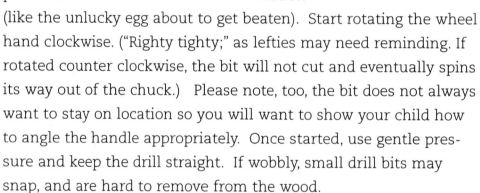

Cost: $35-40

Description: Aptly named, this drill looks and acts like an old-fashioned eggbeater. The handle at top is for holding and steering, the hand wheel at the side drives the drill. The hand-operated chuck at the bottom holds the drill bits.

Use: Hold the drill like an eggbeater and position the drill bit at the desired location (like the unlucky egg about to get beaten). Start rotating the wheel hand clockwise. ("Righty tighty;" as lefties may need reminding. If rotated counter clockwise, the bit will not cut and eventually spins its way out of the chuck.) Please note, too, the bit does not always want to stay on location so you will want to show your child how to angle the handle appropriately. Once started, use gentle pressure and keep the drill straight. If wobbly, small drill bits may snap, and are hard to remove from the wood.

Care: Hand drills are remarkably durable. Reasonable care in any desired storage will do. Make sure to place the bits straight in the chuck, and try to avoid opening too far as they can fall apart as they age and can be hard to reassemble, especially when the chuck jaw springs get bent.

DRILL BITS

Cost: $3-5 each

Description: Useful sizes for this sort of work are 1/4-inch, 5/16-inch 3/8-inch, and 1/2-inch. Smaller bits snap very easily in the hands of wobbly, novice drillers. Anything bigger is too hard to turn with the hand drill. Make sure the drill shanks are 1/4-inch to fit the drill chuck; others can be bought separately, as needed.

SCREWDRIVER

Cost: $10 - $30

Description: When considering screwdrivers think of a basic set –
usually two Phillips (cross-shaped tip) and three with common
square-bladed tips. The variety of common screwdriver sizes is
almost endless, but Phillips are better defined by actual sizes —
#1 and #2 being the most useful. Basic screwdriver sets are most
useful for starters.

Use: Generally, screwdrivers are used for installing and removing
screws such as those in hinges. Eventually the fascination of a
hinged door on a project will be irresistible, so knowing how to
start a screw is worthwhile if not essential.

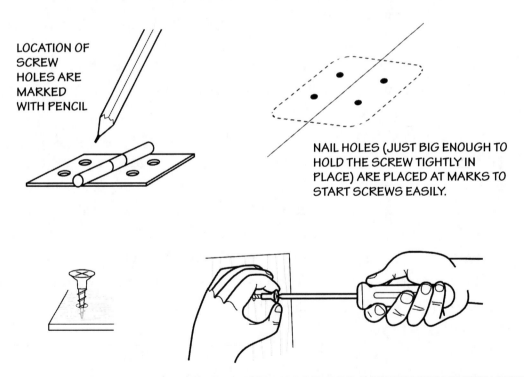

LOCATION OF
SCREW
HOLES ARE
MARKED
WITH PENCIL

NAIL HOLES (JUST BIG ENOUGH TO
HOLD THE SCREW TIGHTLY IN
PLACE) ARE PLACED AT MARKS TO
START SCREWS EASILY.

INSERT THE SCREW IN THE HOLE, BALANCE WITH TWO FINGERS OF
ONE HAND AND TURN GENTLY CLOCKWISE ("RIGHTLY-TIGHTY") WITH
OTHER HAND UNTIL IT GRABS HOLD OF THE WOOD, AND YOU CAN
TURN IT THE REST OF THE WAY IN WITH THE SCREWDRIVER

INTRODUCTION TO PROJECTS

Start Simply

Here comes the good stuff! Now you have the tools and work-space, it is time to decide what to do. Kids love making things, taking charge of their ideas, and experiencing the thrill of success. And who does not? The process of planning and making a project should teach much more than just the value of hard work. The best part about it: children have a wonderful time woodworking and don't realize they are learning important life skills along the way. As parents and teachers, we can make sure this happens. By the time children have completed a project they have had to look hard at their initial plans and ideas, work on their hand skills, face frustration, and test their commitment. They will have pushed themselves and found out how much they care. We need to make sure they look at their choices and decisions every step of the way, and they need to believe they can succeed: Failure is not an option, and quitting is a terrible mistake.

Above all, woodworking should be a pleasurable experience, and a bold challenge. This is where we grown-ups come in. We want to guide a child toward projects within his or her grasp. A person who can barely hold a hammer is not going to attempt to build a Queen Anne lowboy. Someday, perhaps, but for now let's acquire the basic skills and enjoy the progress we make from starting simple. As the projects in It Wood be Fun are arranged in order of difficulty, beginning with the simplest, the book gives parents and children a built-in guide.

But even before looking at the projects, you can encourage young children to work with small scraps of soft wood, obtainable at cabinet shops, lumberyards, or woodworking facilities. I recommend simple assembly with nails, cutting, shaping, and creating imaginary things such as a cell phone from a small, smoothed rectangle, a boat from a small piece of wood nailed onto a larger piece, a bird or an airplane with "wings" attached to a narrow strip. Random assembly or cutting can produce interesting shapes that become whatever a child wants: creatures, trucks, trains, or space stations.

Kids get innovative and creative without much if any prodding. Your job is to set the stage for such playful engagement with wood on a child's own terms. How do you do this? By creating a practical work and storage area, and then by stepping back to allow your child a chance to make his or her first tentative (and later bolder, more self-assured) forays into using the tools and materials. Needless to say, this is a fine line to walk, because your interested and engaged presence remains vital. By gently urging and encouraging good workmanship and follow through, such as sanding and a coat of paint and shellac, you help your child achieve the kind of satisfying result that sustains interest and pride.

For kids this kind of low-key beginning works very well. As skills and confidence grow, and children "age" in the process, the allure of a "real" project will take over. Here adults can help their children decide where and how to start.

Attitude

Perhaps the most important part of these early projects involves attitude. Professional is a favorite word of mine. I say things like: "Professionals don't like rubber nails and coming out parties on their projects. They like silky smooth edges and nice paint jobs. No holidays." I like to see the kids always reaching — looking to be the best they can be. It can be a delicate balance between enjoyment and creativity versus discipline, expectation, and conscious skill development.

Encouragement works wonders. You can help children see they

have the capacity to accomplish what they set out to do by saying things like,

"You're terrific, show the world you are — put it out there!"

"Go for wonderful; don't settle for average when you can be outstanding!" Kids *are* wonderful and they will go the distance. We need to expect that.

The following projects, generated by children and sure to please, represent great stepping off places only – a way to start. Kids have a marvelous capacity to come up with their own ideas. We need to support their creativity. One project often leads to another, and any and all can be a medium for nurturing greatness.

Fantasy Projects

Especially for the youngest or most inexperienced children, working with small wood scraps can help introduce them to woodworking in a natural way. It is especially important to refrain from time restraints and expectations for a particular outcome or product. Expect to spend several sessions or more on such creative exploration, depending on how far your child's imagination ranges, before he wants to move on. Skills can develop as needed, confidence can grow, and perhaps most important, imagination can flower.

Even here, you can help your child develop a work ethic and a taste for quality and refinements. You can suggest adding a smoke stack to a tug boat, say, or a propeller — anything that will stretch a child's skills but keep him or her well within the realm of the doable and fun. In addition, you can stress finish work, such as smoothing edges, and neat, careful painting. All these things stretch a child's imagination and add to the joy of success and accomplishment.

Time

Older children may want to know how long a project will take. I am so often asked, "Mr. Bentinck-Smith, how long will it take? Will it be done today?" I work hard to avoid such questions because I want my people to concentrate on the job, do the best they can, enjoy the process and not worry about how long it takes.

I often say, "You have time — go be wonderful."

"Do you want this project? If you do, we will manage the time and get through it together."

Unfortunately (and often realistically) parents may need to have some idea how long a project will take. This can be a tough call as two factors are always at play: how capable is the child, and how strong is his or her motivation? In addition, putting time restraints on a project all too often creates unnecessary discouragement and reasons to fail.

Yet, sometimes we have to deal with deadlines: "I want to make something for grandpa for his birthday." Maybe that's tomorrow! What do we do? This calls for an assessment. "Practice" projects or experimenting with the tools can help you gauge a child's skills in light of his or her ambitions. Generally, I suggest starting slowly. If you have any doubts or questions about a child's capacity; far better to plan for more time rather than less. Age plays a part, too. A five-year-old will seldom concentrate longer than 25 to 30 minutes, but a ten-year old can well handle an hour at a whack. When possible, try to think in "bites of time," "installments," or "steps" when planning a project. This helps kids realize the value of carry over and hanging in there — rather like making bread when we have to proceed step by step, waiting for the milk to cool and the yeast to rise before moving onto the next phase.

In the realm of practice and experimentation, the "fantasy" project is a good testing ground for figuring out how quickly and accurately a child can perform, especially the younger ones. These projects fit nicely into time slots such as those 40 minutes waiting for the pie to come out of the oven, or for a friend to visit. Fantasy projects have an organic nature, too. They can be whatever your child wants and as simple or complex as his skills and temperament allow.

Many of the more advanced projects in this book also have the capacity for modification through adding or subtracting accessories. The basic project can lead to something more complicated as the graphic organizer in the directions section will indicate.

I have attempted to approximate the minimum time needed to accomplish many of the projects in this book. It is as hard to gauge accurately as it is to say how much time it will take to peel ten apples. (I can do this fast but I know some who could take all morning.) Skill level, concentration, and motivation vary. My time predictions reflect the past performance of children in woodwork classes. Use these estimates to get a general idea. And just remember, whenever possible, I urge children (and adults) to shed time constraints in favor of the joy and wonder of the process at hand.

Safety

Working with hand tools as opposed to power lessens but does not negate safety issues. I have occasionally been asked about safety glasses or goggles for children using tools. When using hand tools with soft wood, there is minimal need for eye protection. You can wear plastic glasses to protect your eyes, but glasses can get dirty or scratched and impair vision, making accidents and injuries more likely.

There is a difference between care, caution, and paranoia. Getting too caught up in the possibility of getting hurt simply breeds fear. People (especially small ones) who are afraid simply can't take any risks, can't perform, and won't grow from the experience. I make no judgments or recommendations other than care and common sense. Tired, angry, or impatient and inattentive people don't perform well or safely. Feeling confident, enthusiastic, and interested in successful results go a long way toward staying safe.

Ultimately, it's up to you. If eye protection, gloves, well-fitting aprons, or face masks make you feel safe, use them. There is no magic formula or perfect answer. You may also want to remind your child, "Tools are not toys." "Real tools can cause real accidents." "Tools are only as safe as the people using them." In all my years of teaching, classroom accidents were minor and remarkably few: an occasional small cut, scratch, bruised thumb, and dusty eyes or mouth.

Challenging Moments

We all have moments of frustration and fatigue. When children hit that wall, you may hear things like: "I can't." "I'm sick of this," or "I'm tired." Take your cues from the tone of voice and look more than the words, and try taking a short break, having a snack, using a fresh approach, or simply putting tools and materials away for another day. Since quitting is a choice, we want to help children stay on the job and experience the pleasure of success. Ways to do this include demonstrating, assisting with problem solving, and offering encouragement (sometimes even gentle pushing). Suggesting a small child choke up on the hammer handle, for example, or remembering the "pull back, pull back" mantra with the handsaw may be all that's needed to curtail frustration and keep a child going.

Beware of performing the skill for your child, however; that dilutes the frustration, but leaves a child feeling helpless. Demonstrate or talk your child through a difficulty, if need be, and then encourage him or her to master it and move on. (I used to tell my students I was willing to help but I didn't do work for people:

When you hear a child say "I can't" you can comeback kindly with, "Show me how you can't do it." "Not bad for someone who can't." Pretty soon they are going full tilt again.) The real victory for children is realizing they can do more than they realize.

What about the child who gets mad? Abuses tools? Spoils work? Anger is also inevitable. Nobody likes to be frustrated, injured, unsuccessful in their efforts, but it happens to us all. Managing anger is an important skill that can be learned. When we are mad, we start to lose it. Our patience goes; our thought process is impaired, impulsive, and ineffective. What to do at this point? Again, take a break and try again later. Developing patience is a part of the process.

What about the child who refuses to use the tools correctly: repeatedly breaking the coping saw blades, for example. They break when the saw is forced, not kept straight, or rushed. I had a rule that only one blade was allowed per period. When the second blade broke, the student couldn't use a coping saw the rest of the period. The same sort of rules can apply to improper or unsafe use of all the other tools. "Use it right or don't use it." Kids learn fast that tools are lots of fun and can do great things but require care, correct handling, and seriousness.

A work ethic matters too. All too often, kids will go after the quick fix. "Oh, it is good enough for me." We need to bring that up short in a hurry with questions like the following:

"That's all you can give to that?"

"A great idea, and that's all?"

"Don't you want it to look like a real tugboat?"

"How come you don't want your project to look wonderful?"

"That's pretty good, but that's it?"

Whatever it takes to help the child put out, do it. Don't encourage lack of effort. Shoddy workmanship is not beautiful. Real success with anything takes real endeavor. Children need to get used to this, just as we need to watch the effort they put into something and to balance our responses in a way that will encourage rather than discourage. Some kids have natural talent, skills come easily; others do not. Those who don't should get encouragement and support when what they have done shows effort, commitment, and dedication. Success will always come to those who dig into a project. Even talented people leave success behind if they don't work.

How about injuries? Learning to start a nail cannot be done without hammering one's thumb or finger at least once; starting a saw often results in scratches; plane-, chisel-, and knife-handling can cause cuts. Hand tool accidents are not life threatening. Running cold water over a bruised thumb; washing and applying Band-Aids to a cut and a dose of sympathy usually take care of the problem. After which, it is important to keep going. These incidents are like mouthfuls of water when learning to swim or scratches and bruises when first on a bicycle – grounds for discomfort and hesitation, surely, which teach us new respect for the skill, but not grounds for quitting.

Each step, each difficulty, each challenge is a teachable moment. Every child has to face his or her hesitation and move beyond. Parents offer the crucial support and encouragement that help a child move forward, help her see success is within reach. We are all made of the right stuff. We just need to believe it. Help your child keep reaching by making the goals realistic. Each success whets the appetite for another. Few things do more for self-assurance and self-esteem.

Getting Started (or Off and Running)

"What do you want to make?"

"An ocean cruiser"

"Good idea, but could we make it a bit smaller?"

"How about a sailboat, instead?"

"Well...."

"Okay, how about a motor boat?"

"Great."

Children need guidance, tempering, and direction. Following their ideas with enthusiasm is very important, but not at the risk of certain failure. When in doubt start slowly, and keep it simple!

Sometimes a child cannot come up with an idea. Maybe she lacks confidence; maybe he just can't get it together. Here's where you might step in and suggest, "How about trying a tool?" This often sparks an idea, a fantasy project that gets your child started. (Off to the wood scrap collection; out come the hammer and nails.)

TRICKS OF THE TRADE

As with any craft, we all start off doing things by the book, following all the rules, and eventually we find and develop our own invaluable shortcuts, and certain idiosyncratic ways of doing things. Here are a few time saving techniques and approaches to woodworking with children I have discovered over the years.

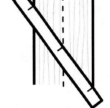

IN HALF

DIVIDING BOARDS WITH A RULER:

It is always best to mark divisions in two places on the board and draw cut lines along these points prior to sawing. Boards are seldom evenly divisible by anything, by the way, and thus following precise measurements for projects in this book is less important than establishing the proper relationship between each part to the whole. When cutting several lengths of the same width strip from a board, you can tip the ruler to divide the board into the desired number of

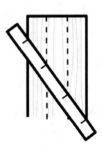

IN THIRDS

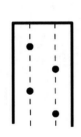

MARK DIVISIONS IN TWO PLACES AND DRAW LINES

pieces. Do this in two or three separate places on the board, to assure accuracy of your lines and cuts.

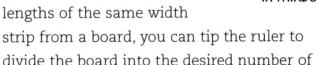

SQUARE

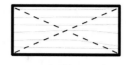

RECTANGLE

ODD
FOUR-
SIDED
SCRAP

FINDING THE CENTER OF A FOUR-SIDED FIGURE

Draw lines between diagonally opposite corners to locate the center. This is especially useful for making circles as big as possible.

HOMEMADE COMPASS:

Find the center, as recommended above, and start a nail at that point. The nail should be secure but easily removable. Tie a string to a pencil. Tie the other end in loop around the nail, adjusting to closest edge of board (for the largest circle possible) and draw with pencil. Don't forget to let the string turn or follow the pencil, or like a dog on a rope circling a tree, the string will wrap about the nail, and your circle will start to shrink!

"CROSS THE VISE TRICK"

Used for starting nails in round stock (dowels, for example)

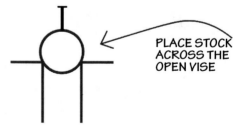

START NAIL AT THE TOP

PLACE STOCK ACROSS THE OPEN VISE

a.   Open vise about half the width of the stock.

b.   Place stock across the open vise.

c.   Starting a nail will be a breeze as the round stock will stay put, not roll or squeeze down into the vise. Start nail at top.

CUT A CIRCLE IN THE BOARD

a)   Drill small hole (1/4-inch to 1/2-inch will do) somewhere along the circumference

b)   Remove the blade from the coping saw, thread through the hole, and then replace in the saw.

c)   Cut out the hole, remove the blade and coping saw, and smooth as needed. This saves you from having to make a saw cut through the edge of the board to reach the hole.

PATTERN MAKING

When you want to draw a symmetrical object such as a heart, a circle, a boat, or a square, try this approach:

a) Fold a piece of paper in half after deciding how big you want the whole.

b) Draw desired half shape on the piece of paper, taking care the folded edge is on the inside.

c)   Leaving paper folded, cut out, unfold, and voila!

PROJECT ASSEMBLY

Project parts are much easier to assemble if nails are started first. With 1-inch wood such as I recommend using, it's best to start nails 3/8-inch from the edge. You will soon be able to guess the 3/8-inch distance, but I always mark "X's" for a child to start with. I usually hold the parts and start the assembly to make sure the wood matches up well and fits together properly. Small children are simply not strong or big enough to do this. As there will probably be plenty of imperfections, a loose fit and wobbly assembly should not be among them. The kids always complete the job with gusto and enthusiasm.

SAVE WOOD SCRAPS

Cutting chair and table legs and other pieces for the following projects, you'll generate a lot of scrap wood. Save decent sized scraps! There is no end of uses for these bits and pieces. The car's wheels, for example, can be cut from scrap, as can add-ons, embellishments, and cleats. As with sewing and other handcrafts, thrift with materials (which means saving leftovers) pays off.

In addition, if you have a toddler in the house, wood scraps, like wooden spools, make great gluing projects.

CUTOUTS

Let's take a minute to look at simple cutouts to embellish any of the projects in this book. Here's the prototypical cutout project.

Ability Level: Basic-Intermediate

Materials:

- One 16-inch 1 x 8 pine board

Tools:

- Vise
- Coping saw
- Four-way combination rasp

Description: This is a project of unlimited subject matter. I suggest parents and teachers keep the drawing as simple as possible, as at first you will need to guide the idea into reality. If a child wants to cutout a boat, for example, sketch a top or side view, which he can cut out easily. If she wants a cutout of an animal, make the legs thick and the body as large as possible; keep the overall shapes clear and uncluttered to minimize damage to the saw and the outcome. Coloring books can provide traceable images.

Steps:

1. Your child chooses a subject
2. You and your child draw the subject on a board. Simplify the details when possible!

3. Draw so that one side or point of entry touches an edge.

4. Place the board in the vise and using the coping saw, cut out the shape. Don't forget to move the board as needed to facilitate cutting. Remember: Vises are only as good as the people using them! Help kids realize that thinking about this is intelligent tool use.

5. Smooth edges as needed

6. Paint as desired — your kids will want to decide and help with paint mixing and brushing — let them!

Comments:

A cutout can be a project totally unto itself, hung on the wall as a decoration, a statement (such as a heart), or a label. Or a cutout can be incorporated into another project, such as the bookshelf, chair, book ends, and so on, as an embellishment. It can be complex or ultra-simple. Even the simplest cutout helps a child learn to plan ahead, sketch out an idea, and handle a coping saw. As I tell the children in my classes, practice makes better!

Platform

We begin with the simplest project, which will be a lot of fun and a good challenge for a child new to woodworking. As you move along through the book, you will notice the projects get increasingly more complex, exciting, and time-consuming. In each case, note the ability level and materials needed before launching in; it's frustrating to run out of an essential part or to realize you lack the proper tools or skills halfway through a project. Rather like discovering you have no eggs after melting the butter and chocolate for making brownies.

Ability Level: Basic

Time: 1/4 to 1/2 hour

Materials:

- Two 16-inch lengths of 1 x 8 pine
- Two cleats (strips of pine 8 to 10-inches long, 1- to 2-inches wide) used to attach the boards together
- 6d 2-inch finish nails

Tools:

- Hammer

Description: The basic platform is the launching point for castles, airports, battle stations, ball fields, golf courses, maps, checker boards, shields, desk covers, and any other wonderful idea that comes to mind, that utilizes a 16-inch square. This is the first step down the path to future woodworking greatness!

Steps:

1. Mark cleats for starting nails — three nails in each board is best but two will probably do if the cleat is too short. Let you child or student start the nails.

2. Position 16-inch-long boards on top of two matched 1 x 8,

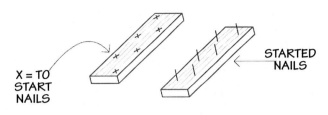

X = TO START NAILS

STARTED NAILS

16-boards. (Parents, you may want to lend a hand by holding boards tightly together and perhaps starting nails and driving them through the cleats and into the 1 x 8's as well. Kids can carry on nicely thereafter, just do continue to hold together tightly to minimize the space (or crack) between the boards – this makes the platform look and work better.

3.   Nail cleats and clinch the nails hard on top for a smooth surface. Clinching is bending over the protruding nail points and hammering them flat into the wood.

4.   When nailing each cleat, make sure the planks and cleats overhang the bench by a little so the nails won't get stuck in the bench top. Clinch when all nails are in place. Do the same with the second cleat.

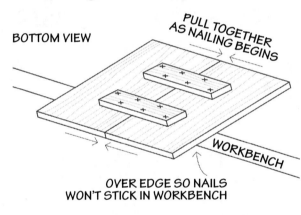

BOTTOM VIEW

PULL TOGETHER AS NAILING BEGINS

WORKBENCH

OVER EDGE SO NAILS WON'T STICK IN WORKBENCH

*Note: Yes, it would be nicer to put the nails the other way down through the top, but it is hard to accurately reach the cleats and the point is to have the kids do as much of the work as possible. We need to accept small losses when working toward the more important goal of teaching skills to complete this first project correctly and well.

By the way, if your child wants to do a checkerboard or other decorative chiseled design, the nails will get in the way. However, kids don't seem to

BOTTOM VIEW

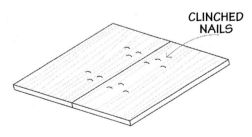

CLINCHED NAILS

mind, and the rewards of this kid of embellishment far outweigh the liabilities.

SAMPLE POSSIBILITIES ORIGINATING FROM THE BASIC PLATFORM

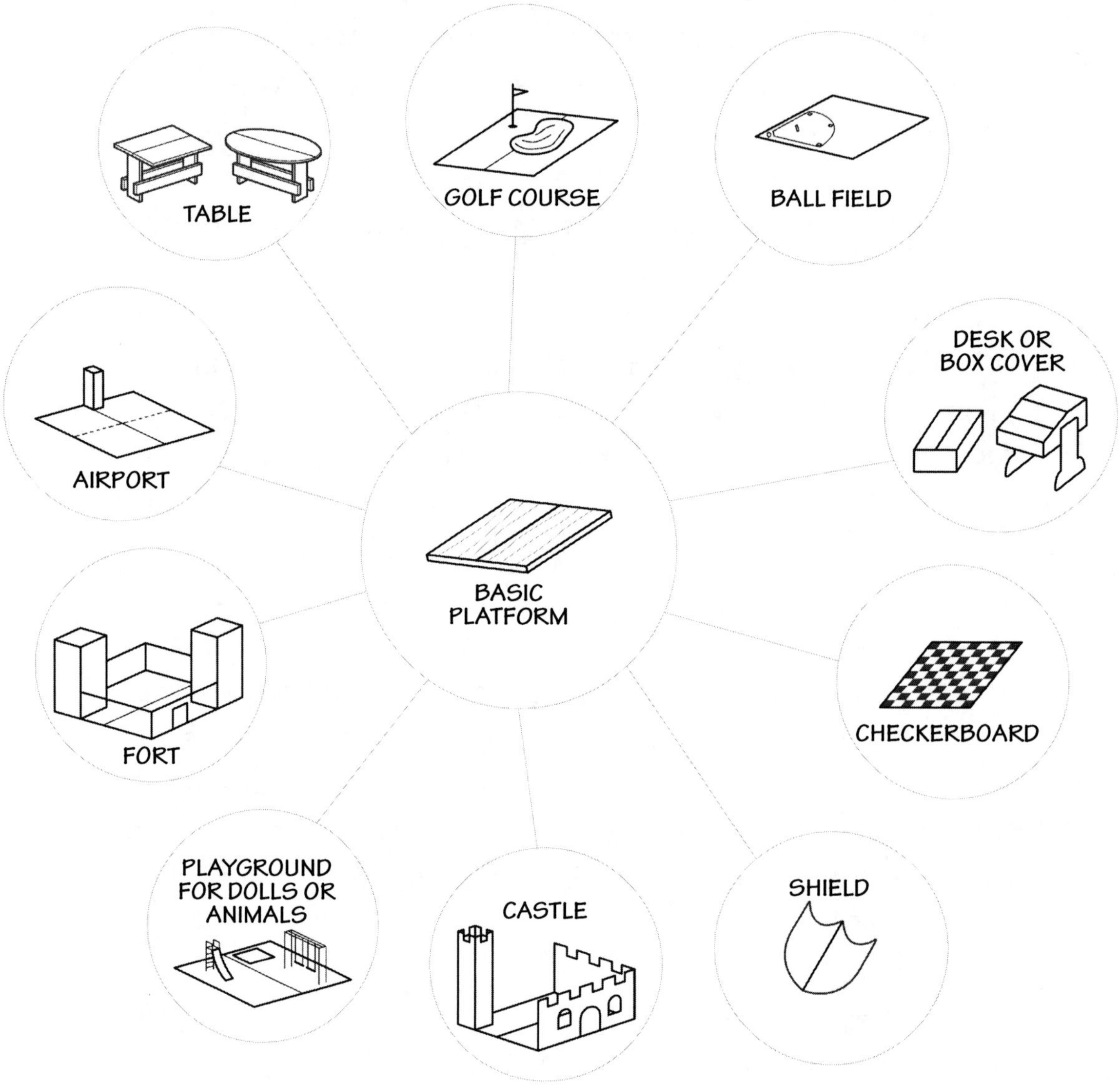

TABLE

GOLF COURSE

BALL FIELD

DESK OR BOX COVER

AIRPORT

BASIC PLATFORM

CHECKERBOARD

FORT

SHIELD

PLAYGROUND FOR DOLLS OR ANIMALS

CASTLE

Sign

Ability Level: Basic

Time: 1/2 hour minimum

Materials needed:

- 1 16-inch length of 1 x 8 clear pine (knots are hard to carve)

Tools:

- C-clamp
- Chisel
- Hammer

Description: Signs can say anything. The easiest are ones with initials or short words like Mom and Dad written in large letters on one line. More lines, smaller letters, are harder to carve.

Steps:

1. You will want to draw block letters on the board, unless your child can do this. Two lightly drawn parallel lines help

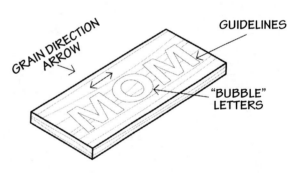

keep the letters the same size and straight: Write using a single line, then "bubble" it, so the letters can be carved. Fasten the board to the work table with a C-clamp.

2. Remind your child to always carve with the grain (lengthwise in this case). After down-cutting the outline to define the letter's edge, have your child use a chisel to hollow it out. Remember to suggest holding the bevel side toward the edge for better carving.

3. When letters are chiseled, sand the edges "silky smooth."

4.   Paint the letters first — no holidays or gaps in the paint— to make the background behind the letters easier to paint. Encourage the use of different colors for a dynamic, creative sign.

Comments: This project offers a good chiseling experience.

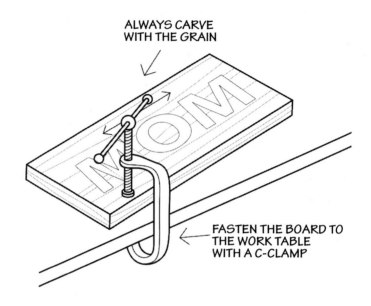

ALWAYS CARVE WITH THE GRAIN

FASTEN THE BOARD TO THE WORK TABLE WITH A C-CLAMP

Children can learn what happens if they are too heavy handed – the letters get trashed with escaped chisel activity. It gives children a chance to decorate, convey a personal message, mark a house (their own house or a doll's house) with a number or name, designate where they hang coats in the front hall or put their toys (with luck!) at the end of the day!

Boat

Ability level: Basic

Time: 1/2 to 1 hour-plus

Materials:

- One to two lengths of
  1 x 8 pine
- String
- 6d 2-inch finish nails
- 4d 1 1/2-inch finish nails
- Rubber band
- Thin strip of wood or a dowel
  (for mast or paddle)
- Paper or cloth (for the sail
  and flag)

Tools:

- Vise
- Scissors
- Pencil
- Thick dowels
  (for smokestacks
  or guns)
- Four-way combination rasp

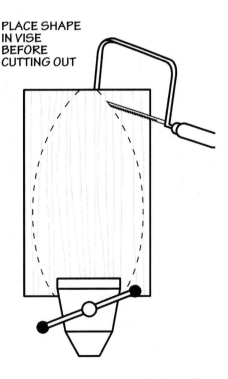

**PLACE SHAPE
IN VISE
BEFORE
CUTTING OUT**

Description: The basic boat shape is a piece of cake — just draw, cut out, and smooth. Then comes the part where your child can use his imagination to embellish the boat: a fence around the edges, a mast, a cabin, smokestacks, guns, and a garage for the tank have all been popular add-ons. "What would you like?" I always ask. "It's your boat!"

Steps:

1.   Using a pattern or careful sketch, draw out a boat shape filling as much of the board as possible. (Larger boats lend themselves best to the add-ons but smaller boats have appeal as well.) Cut out with the coping saw and smooth with the sandpaper block.

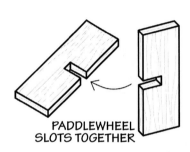

PADDLEWHEEL
SLOTS TOGETHER

2.   If a paddle is desired, cut a slot about 2-inches wide at the stern. For a large boat, each paddle half will need to be 2-3-inches long by 1-1/2 inches wide. The two paddle blades will need to interlock.

3.   Place one small nail on each side of the slot, place the rubber band on the paddle assembly and stretch across the slot onto each nail. (When the boat is done, one can wind the paddle and it will churn through the water like the Mississippi Queen.)

4.   The railing or "fence" consists of a row of nails along the gunwale (edge) about 1-1/2 inches apart with string wrapped around each and tied at the end. Rub a drop of glue onto each wrap, especially the knot at the end to prevent untying. (Kids

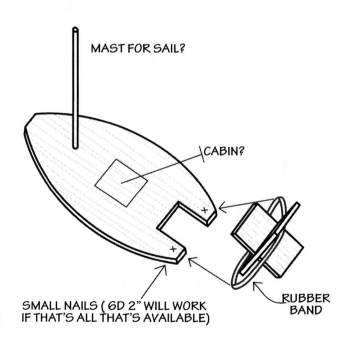

MAST FOR SAIL?

CABIN?

RUBBER BAND

SMALL NAILS (6D 2" WILL WORK IF THAT'S ALL THAT'S AVAILABLE)

often don't like tying this knot but they don't like tying shoes either. Encourage perseverance!)

5.   The mast can be carved from a strip with the sloyd knife or planed round with a block plane or you can use a dowel cut to the desired length. Large boats require about a 3/8-inch dowel — drill a hole at the desired location on the boat, and glue in the mast. For the sail, cut a triangle to the desired size and shape from paper or cloth and glue onto the mast.

6.   Cabins or garages are basically boxes of any size or shape — a solid or hollow block nailed on to hold a tank, car, beanie baby, stuffed animal, or whatever needs a ride. Cut the roof of the box from wood scraps. What shape should this be? Here's another important decision the builder must make.

Smokestacks are most easily attached to the cabin before attaching it to the boat.

The basic boat lends itself to further details. Each boat will reflect the whims and desires of the creator. This is a great opportunity to encourage some independent thinking, and to read stories or look at picture books featuring boats. If your child's interest really sparks, you might visit a local harbor or shipyard, if possible.

Box

Ability level: Basic

Time: 1/2 hour plus

Materials:

- Six sixteen-inch lengths of 1 x 8 pine
- 6d 2-inch finish nails

Tools:

- Four-way combination rasp
- Hammer

Optional:

- Handsaw
- Vise

BEGIN WITH TWO EQUALLY SIZED PIECES OF PINE, AND START FOUR NAILS ON EACH END.

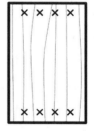

Description: This is an easily accomplished project with multiple uses. It can house toys, a rock collection or some other treasure. It can be used for imaginative play with cars and trucks, or for the garage on the boat project.

Steps:

1. Lay out two equal 1 x 8 pieces of pine. Start four nails at each end, 3/8-inch from the edge.

2. One at a time, nail the boards at a 90-degree angle to two more pieces (A and B) of 1 x 8's. Small children especially need help holding the wood to align the pieces properly. The box will not look good and it will be difficult to nail if the corners and edges are not lined up. Nails gone awry are called "a coming out party." They will make the edges look crooked and lumpy.)

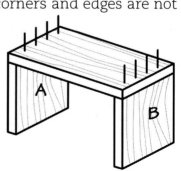

3. Fit two more pieces <u>inside</u> the box for the bottom. The boards will fit only in one direction. (If too long, choose

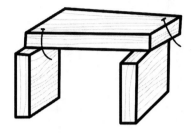

another board when possible, or file or plane to fit, remembering the "cross grain" planing technique. If too wide, one board can be planed with the grain until it fits.)

4. The bottom will have to be nailed in from the outside, one board at a time, with the nails placed 3/8-inch from the edge. (ABCD, below) After the boards are nailed at the ends, use five nails to secure them along each side.

5. Do be aware these boards will likely not be wide enough to cover the bottom if you choose to nail on outside. You may need to cut an additional strip to complete the bottom.

Another caveat: You will want to make sure the nails are completely hammered in to avoid scratching the floor or table.

WIDE

LONG

6. After smoothing the edges with the four-way combination rasp, your child may want to paint his box for a handsome, finished look.

Comments: The basic box structure lends itself to many other possibilities. It can be the start of a bookshelf, doll-house, parking garage, jail, and cat box. When your child is familiar with the process, she can easily conceive and add embell-ishments or whatever her imagination and newfound skills suggest.

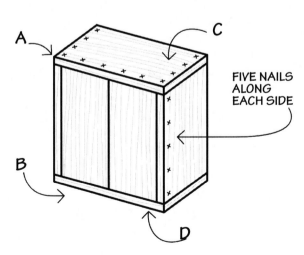

A
B
C
D
FIVE NAILS ALONG EACH SIDE

BOOKSHELF

DOLLHOUSE

CUPBOARD

BASIC BOX

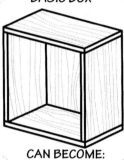

CAN BECOME:

CATBOX

GARAGE

JAIL

CAGE

Bookshelf

Ability level: Basic

Time: 1/2 hour

Materials:

- Five 16-inch lengths of 1 x 8 pine
- Handful of 6d 2-inch finish nails

Tools:

- Hammer
- Try square
- Pencil

Description: This is simple 16-inch-square bookshelf consisting of three shelves and two side pieces. Assembly with nails is the only construction step, there is no sawing involved.

Steps:

1. Match as best possible — three identical bookshelf lengths, and two identical side lengths

2. Find the center of each of the two side lengths, and mark using the try square.

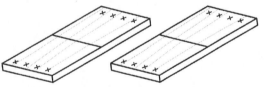

FIND CENTER OF EACH SIDE LENGTH AND MARK WITH TRY SQUARE

3. At each end of these two matching side pieces, your child will start four nails, 3/8-inch in from the ends, and four nails at the center line.

4. Line up the three identical shelf boards end to end with the nail points at the top, middle, and bottom of the side boards. You may want to hold and hammer the nails partway through the shelves to get a straight start, but your child can

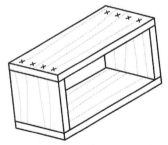

ASSEMBLE SIDES, TOP AND BOTTOM, LIKE AN OPEN BOX

(and should) complete the nailing.

5.   Do check for "rubber" nails and "coming out parties" — nails that come out of the wood slanted, and replace as needed with new nails in new locations. Again, this is all about learning, so do be patient if you have to help your child drive a straight nail. It takes practice!

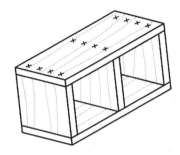

A. START FOUR NAILS ON CENTER LINE OF SIDES

B. SLIDE IN AND POSITION CENTER SHELF, NAIL ONE SIDE. TURN OVER AND NAIL OTHER SIDE

6.   Smooth and sand the corners and edges in preparation to paint.

7.   Poster paint gives a good finish to the bookshelf. Remember to watch for "holidays" — gaps in the painted surface. The broad flat surfaces of the bookshelf lend themselves to painted designs, pictures, names, and so on.

Shield

Ability Level: Basic-Intermediate

Time: 1/2 hour plus

Materials:

- Two 16-inch lengths of 1 x 8 pine
- 6d 2-inch finish nails
- Scraps for cleats and handle

Tools:

- Vise
- Coping saw
- Hammer
- Four-way combination rasp
- Handsaw
- Block Plane

Description: This project starts with the basic platform, with the shape of the shield anything that can be drawn on it.

Steps:

1.   After the platform is built, draw the desired shape for the shield on the platform (with boards running vertically):

Discourage your child from doing just a square as this looks sort of crude and is a quick fix, by saying something like: "Why not make it look like a real shield?" (You might want to look at pictures of shields and knights in armor to extend the discussion of possibilities and to pique your child's interest.)

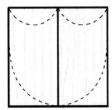 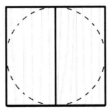 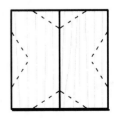

2.   Cut out the desired shape with the handsaw, and smooth the edges (with a block plane or four-way combination rasp) to a comfortable roundness.

3.   Add a handle between cleats on the back. Now your child might want to go a step further to design a coat of arms to paint or chisel into the wood before applying a coat of paint. (Try a silver metallic paint for this project to add glamour and authenticity.)

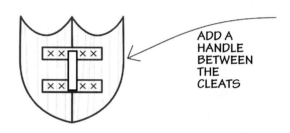

ADD A HANDLE BETWEEN THE CLEATS

Comments: This is a straightforward project that invites creative thinking. The shields are great for snowball fights and playacting, but even if children never use them, they simply love the idea of having a shield. You can hang it on the workshop or bedroom wall, and augment by reading age-appropriate tales of knights in armor.

In fact, any of the projects in this book can become springboards for further engagement through storytelling, reading, research in children's encyclopedias or online, imaginative play, field trips, and artwork. Perhaps your child will cut out a simple medieval tunic to wear with his shield, decide to make a helmet and sword, or enjoy a visit to a local armory museum, if within reach. Or, perhaps she will develop a lifelong interest in the Middle Ages! You can never anticipate or predict what will spark a child's imagination, but you can be on the lookout, ready to encourage an interest, or satisfy an eagerness to learn more.

Bookends

Ability level: Basic-Intermediate

Time: 1/2 hour plus

Materials:

• Two 16-inch length 1 x 8's

Tools:

• Hammer

• Try square

• Vise

• 6 d finish nails

• Four-way combination rasp

• Handsaw and coping saw

Description: These simple L-shaped bookends will hold a row of books straight on a table or on a shelf. The side faces can be decorated before starting or after finishing the bookends.

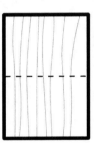 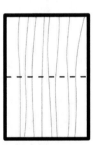

SAW CAREFULLY AT THE 8" MARK

Steps:

1. Find the center of the 16-inch long board at the 8-inch point and draw a line with the try square for cutting. Saw as carefully as possible.

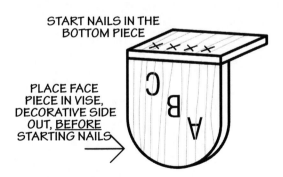

START NAILS IN THE BOTTOM PIECE

PLACE FACE PIECE IN VISE, DECORATIVE SIDE OUT, <u>BEFORE</u> STARTING NAILS

2. Mark 3/8-inch on one end of each of the two pieces, with four points (X's) evenly spaced for starting nails.

3. Start nails in the bottom piece and attach to

the face pieces making sure the decorations (if done prior to putting the bookends together) face out! Make sure the nails are completely driven home to avoid scratching surfaces later.

Note: Put the face piece in the vise, decorative side out before attaching bottom piece.

4.   Finish the edges with the four-way combination rasp until they are "silky smooth."

5.   Encourage the use of color and decoration as desired — do let your child choose the colors, and remind him, "Professional painters use one color at a time."

Comments: Basic bookends are certainly useful, but you can also consider them a wonderful opportunity for developing a flair with creative embellishments. You might encourage your child to change the shape of the top edge of the exposed faces, to carve a design or his initials, or to add a small cutout shape in wood or other material. If your child wants to paint the wood – always a terrific option – have her describe or draw what she wants the bookend to look like before starting.

ENCOUARAGE THE USE OF COLOR AND DECORATION AS DESIRED!

This is a small project with a big success rate. Decorating the bookends serves as an excellent stimulus to the imagination. It is important here that kids give their work some thought. Once again, the more effort the more wonderful the result.

Shoes

Ability level: Basic – Intermediate

Time: 1 hour plus

Materials needed:

- 1-2 lengths of 1 x 8 pine
- Piece of rubber (inner tube) or heavy cloth approximately one foot square
- Pencil
- Staple gun and 1/2" staples or heavy (#10) carpet tacks or small nails

Tools:

- Coping saw
- 4-way combination rasp
- Handsaw
- Vise
- Hammer

Description: These are wooden open-toe slip-on-the-foot shoes that delight children. They are comfortable and seem to work well.

Steps:

1.   Trace child's feet in shoes on a piece of 1 x 8. (Small feet will fit on a 1 x 8.)

2.   Cut out shoe "soles" with a coping saw, smooth edges with 4-way combination rasp.

3.   Have child step on "soles" in bare feet, wrap piece of rubber around foot, staple every 3/4". Keep foot in place for four staples — one in each corner for good fit, then remove foot for the rest of the staples—easier on a table than on the floor.

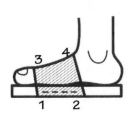

Carpet tacks or nails can replace staples, but are harder to manage. Stapler will require help from an adult.

4.   Paint-on decoration should be sparse, maybe only on the edge of the sole— paint does tend to smudge off on floor and feet!

Comments: This is yet another child-generated idea that really works. The shoes seem to hold up well and can be easily repaired if broken. One small girl wore hers until her foot got too big, which was at the start of high school!

Lamp

Ability level: Basic – Intermediate

Time: 1 hour plus

Materials needed:

- 1-2 lengths of 1 x 8 pine
- Glue
- Pencil
- 6d 2" finish nails
- "Bottle kit"
- Small lampshade that clamps onto lightbulb

Tools:

- Coping saw
- 4-way combination rasp
- Handsaw
- Vise
- Hammer
- 2 C-clamps
- Block plane
- Drill and 3/8" bit

Description: These lamps are not hard to construct, make wonderful bedside or desk lamps, involve some thought and imagination, and are fun to make. Kids love them, and with good reason.

Steps:

1. First part to be made is upright that holds light fixture and to which the base is attached.

2. 3 strips, 2" wide and 8" long need to be cut from a piece of 1 x 8. Make cross cut first, then saw apart.

3. Glue 3 pieces together as closely

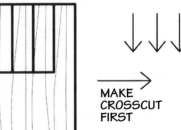

MAKE CROSSCUT FIRST

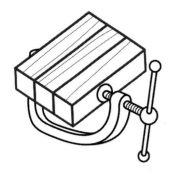

aligned as possible. clamp together and set aside for drying.

4.   Base is next. Base can have an interesting shape. Creativity should be encouraged — a square isn't that exciting.

5.   All the electrical components needed to convert a bottle to a lamp. (The base could complement the attached cutout such as a bird with a round

nest at base.) Possible shapes could be circle, oval, star, kidney bean, etc.

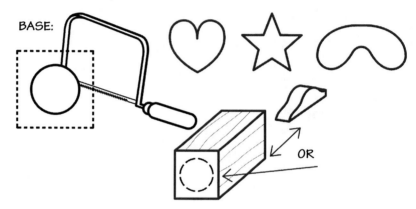

BASE:

OR

Base gets sawed out with coping saw and smoothed with 4-way combination rasp.Make sure base is not too small, so lamp will be stable.

6.   Drill 3/8" hole on one end to receive threaded portion of bottle kit light socket.

3/8" HOLE

7.   Attach base to upright with 2 nails and glue.

8.   Decide on design for applied cutout. Draw shape, cut out with coping saw, and attach to upright with 1 1/2" nails and glue.

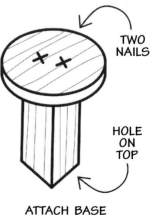

TWO NAILS

HOLE ON TOP

ATTACH BASE

9. Paint or decorate Before attaching bottle kit. Keep it clean and paint-free — it looks better! (Directions on bottle kit package will assist in installation. Eliminate "cork" used in a bottle)

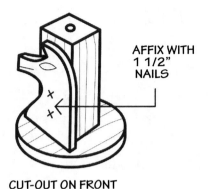

AFFIX WITH 1 1/2" NAILS

CUT-OUT ON FRONT

Comments: This is a project that really works, and can last many years. Kids like the "real deal" sometimes, and this is one of them.

Rocking Horse

Ability level: Basic – Intermediate

Time: 1 to 1 1/2 hours

Materials needed:

- Three 16-inch lengths of 1 x 8 pine
- 6d 2-inch finish nails

Tools:

- Hammer
- Vise
- Handsaw
- Coping saw
- Pencil
- Block plane
- Four-way combination rasp

Description: Here is another small, easily accomplished project that really functions. decorations and finishing touches offer endless possibilities for creativity. The rocking horse provides fun for the builder as well as the user.

Steps:

1.   Bisect lengthwise one piece of 1 x 8 pine for the rockers. Cut on the line with the handsaw.

It is possible to cut out the rockers without bisecting the board, but the work with the coping saw is more manageable if you do.

2.   Now sketch a "rocker" on one of

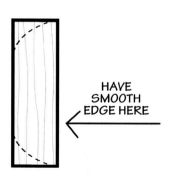

HAVE SMOOTH EDGE HERE

BISECT A PIECE OF 1 X 8 PINE, CUT ON THE LINE WITH HANDSAW

the pieces, and cut out with the coping saw. Smooth the top flat edge.

MAINTAIN CURVE AS PLANING PROGRESSES, AVOID "FLAT TIRE" EFFECT

3.   Trace cut rocker on remaining piece of bisected pine, and again cut out with a coping saw, and smooth.

4.   Match the rockers by placing them together in the vise, and place from the top down. Be sure to maintain the curve as the planing progresses, avoiding a flat-tire look in the center. Planing the rockers this way makes the ride smooth!

5.   Start nails along the sides of another piece of 1 x 8, again set them 3/8-inch in from the edge.

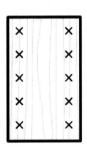

START NAILS AS SHOWN

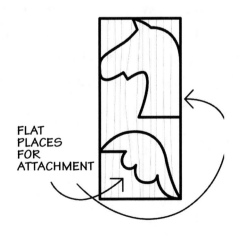

ASSEMBLY IS EASIER IF YOU HOLD EACH ROCKER IN A VISE

6.   Assemble carefully, matching the rockers for evenness. Holding each rocker in a vise makes matching easier.

7.   Sketch the horse's head on one end of another piece of 1 x 8 pine, and the tail on the remaining space. Make sure to leave a flat area at one end of the tail for attachment to the horse's body.

FLAT PLACES FOR ATTACHMENT

START NAILS UNDER
THE PLATFORM OR
BODY OF THE HORSE

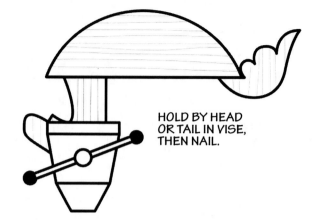

HOLD BY HEAD
OR TAIL IN VISE,
THEN NAIL.

8.   Now cut out both horse head and tail with the coping saw (Depending on your child's age and skill level, this might be something an adult helps with — but here again, perfection is not the issue, rather this is another project where process is more important than product, so long as the rocking horse works and brings delight to the maker, who learns things along the way.) The grain goes lengthwise (from top to bottom) to make the pieces stronger.

9.   Start nails underneath the platform or body of the horse. Place head or tail in the vise, align the horse and nail.

10.   Smooth, paint, and decorate.

Comments: This is a popular project. It makes a wonderful present for a baby brother or sister, and when outgrown, stuffed animals have been known to enjoy riding the rocking horse. Kids love to make things that really work. In addition, this can be a rocking cat or elephant or dog. Leave it up to your child to be inventive. We made a rocking giraffe in class once.

Table

Ability Level: Basic – Intermediate

Time: 1 hour plus

Materials:

- Five 16-inch lengths of 1 x 8 pine
- Two cleats (scraps 8-10-inches long, random widths)
- 6d 2-inch finish nails

Tools:

- Vise
- Handsaw
- Hammer
- Ruler
- Block plane
- Four-way combination rasp

Description: Tables are fun to make and obviously have many uses. Again, it's the functional aspect of a project that captures a child's imagination and endures well beyond the construction phase.

Steps:

1.   Make the top by cleating two pieces of 1 x 8 pine lengths together. Start the nails in the cleats and nail into the two top boards, thus binding them together lengthwise – don't forget to do one cleat at a time and to nail over the edge of the workbench to

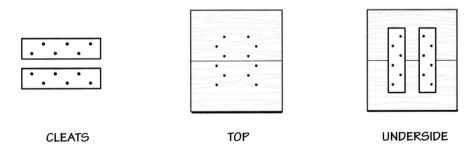

CLEATS   TOP   UNDERSIDE

prevent nails from going into the top. After both cleats are on, clinch nails hard.

2. Start four nails 3/8-inch from the top edge for attaching the legs; two nails on each board close to the split and centered.

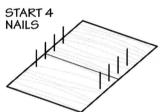

START 4 NAILS

3. Using the nail starts, attach the top to two lengths of 16-inch 1 x 8's, which will be the legs.

4. Bisect lengthwise the remaining piece of 1 x 8, plane sawed edge of each, nail across legs, one on each side to brace legs. Kids like the way this step makes the table strong and useful even though they may not love the sawing.

ATTACH TOP TO TWO LENGTHS OF 1 X 8

ADD BRACES

Comments: If he wants, your child can add a lower shelf by sawing aboard to fit over leg braces. Or she can make a drawer to fit beneath the top. Obviously this takes a bit more skill, patience, and knowhow, but here's where a parent or teacher can step in to help (without taking over). All such additions can be challenging, imaginative, and fun, but the table alone gives a wonderful sense of achievement.

Airplane

Ability Level: Basic – Intermediate

Time: 1 hour plus

Materials:

- One length 1 x 8 pine

Tools:

- Hammer
- 6d 2-inch finish nails
- Drill with 3/8-inch or 1/2-inch bit
- Handsaw
- Pencil
- Coping Saw
- Four-way combination rasp
- Vise
- 1-3/8 chisel and C-clamp

Description: This airplane can be a passenger, transport, or freight plane depending on the needs of the builder. It can have lots of details, and add-ons, or remain bare bones. The basic unit is not complicated, but it can develop into quite a complex project, which will be a lot of fun for an aspiring woodworker-pilot!

Steps:

1.   Three basic parts need to be sketched on the board. You and your child or student will want to decide what the fuselage, wings, and elevator will look like. (see diagram, next page) Now get your child started cutting these pieces out with a coping saw.

2.   Smooth the fuselage, and decide where the wings will go

3.   Mark a slot in the fuselage, drill a hole, and install coping saw to cut out. (see diagram, next page)

4.   Smooth wing slot and the wing, until it slides through easily, then nail in place.

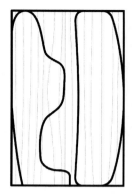

DRAWING WING AND FUSELAGE TOGETHER LIKE THIS MAKES FULL USE OF THE BOARD.

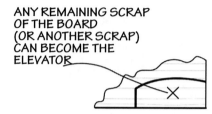

ANY REMAINING SCRAP OF THE BOARD (OR ANOTHER SCRAP) CAN BECOME THE ELEVATOR

5. With or without your help your child will need to draw a small cutout for the elevator at the tail of the plane, fitted to the elevator and nailed in.

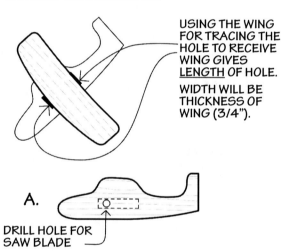

USING THE WING FOR TRACING THE HOLE TO RECEIVE WING GIVES **LENGTH** OF HOLE.

WIDTH WILL BE THICKNESS OF WING (3/4").

A.

DRILL HOLE FOR SAW BLADE

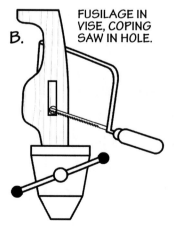

B. FUSILAGE IN VISE, COPING SAW IN HOLE.

6. Guns or jet engines can be round or rounded pieces nailed to wings. Windows can be carved into the sides with a chisel as needed.

A –Using the wing as a guide for the length, trace a hole in the fuselage to secure the wing. The width will be the thickness of the wing, or 3/4-inch.

B – Put the fuselage in the vise; insert the coping blade in the hole ready for cutting.

C – Cut down both sides, then across the

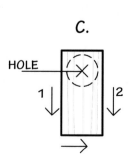

C.

HOLE

1

2

bottom, and the piece will come out easily.

Now smooth the slot or wing surface to help the wing fit into the slot for nailing.

Slide in, center, grip fuselage in the vise, and use two nails to secure it from the underside.

Cut under the fuselage at the wing a slot just deep enough for the elevator to fit in flat and straight. It will get nailed, as well. Try smoothing along the #2 surface to make the elevator straight.

Your child can add guns, bombs, or engine pods to the wing using cut dowels (Check Tricks of the Trade, "cross the vise trick" to start nails easily in a dowel.)

Comments: This project is great once your child has grasped the coping saw skills. It is challenging as well as straightforward and easily tailored to each child's interest. We made lots of them in my woodworking class.

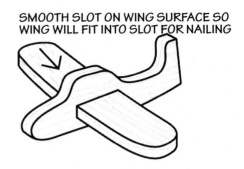

SMOOTH SLOT ON WING SURFACE SO WING WILL FIT INTO SLOT FOR NAILING

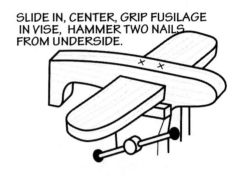

SLIDE IN, CENTER, GRIP FUSILAGE IN VISE, HAMMER TWO NAILS FROM UNDERSIDE.

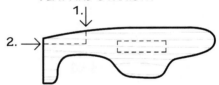

JUST DEEP ENOUGH FOR ELEVATOR TO BE NAILED IN FLAT AND STRAIGHT

SOME SMOOTHING MIGHT BE NEEDED AT #2 SURFACE FOR ELEVATOR TO BE STRAIGHT

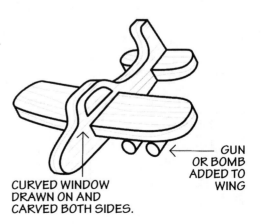

CURVED WINDOW DRAWN ON AND CARVED BOTH SIDES.

GUN OR BOMB ADDED TO WING

Dollhouse

Skill level: Basic – Intermediate

Time: 1 hour at least

Materials:

- Seven (or more) 16-inch lengths of 1 x 8 pine
- 6d 2-inch finish nails
- 4d 1-1/2-inch finish nails

Tools:

- Hammer
- Handsaw
- Coping saw
- Drill, 3/8 bit
- Four-way combination rasp

Steps:

1. The dollhouse starts with the basic bookshelf but before nailing in the shelf or "second floor," your child will want to decide where she wants the staircase, and where to cut the access hole to it.

    A - Center at one end

    B - Center of floor

    C - One side of the end

    a.   Saw down each side with handsaw, and across with the coping saw.

    b.   Drill hole at corner, install coping saw, cutout

    c.   Cut in each side, remove piece

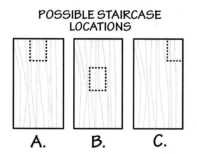

LOCATE THE STAIRCASE

POSSIBLE STAIRCASE LOCATIONS

A.   B.   C.

2. Now, install the second floor

3. Your child will make the staircase from a strip of pine about 2-inches wide by 10- or 11-inches long, the edges planed smooth. Create steps by cutting them out with a hand-saw. (Take care not to cut too deep to avoid break-ing the pine strip.)

BE CAREFUL NOT
TO CUT TOO
DEEPLY

Install staircase as desired.

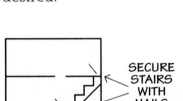

SECURE
STAIRS
WITH
NAILS

4. Most houses have interior walls, this one is no exception. Upstairs and down, measure the space(s) and cut the wall(s) to fit.

5. Decide where you want the door and cut as needed

Position and nail the wall(s). (The bottom of a wall can probably

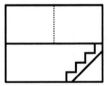

get away with one or two nails, just enough to keep it stable and straight)

6.   If your child wants a pitched roof, he can start by assembling 2 lengths of 1 x 8's, and hammering four nails 3/8-inch in from the edge

 Place roof centered on top, hammer three nails on each edge

Comments: This straightforward dollhouse can generate innumerable ideas. The house can be custom made for whatever doll or animal will live there. Scraps of wallpaper, carpet, and linoleum can decorate walls and cover the floors. Don't forget, however, that the painters leave a job before the interior decorators come in, so encourage your child to paint whatever surfaces she wants first! The exterior, too, can use as much detail as a child wants to undertake. The beauty of this project lies in its open-ended nature.

Chair

Ability level: Intermediate

Time: 1 to 2 hours

Materials:

- Three pieces of 1 x 8 pine
- 6d 2-inch finish nails

Tools:

- Handsaw
- Vise
- Coping saw
- Chisel
- Pencil
- Block plane
- Four-way combination rasp

Description: The chair can be fairly straightforward or detailed, according to the wishes and ambitions of the builder. It makes a great starter project because of its flexibility. As your child progresses through the steps, ideas may spring to mind he can easily incorporate such changing the shape of the back face, carving his name in it, or adding knobs (see Graphic) and so on. Such little touches give the chair character. Suddenly, the chair belongs to its maker in an inimitable way!

Steps:

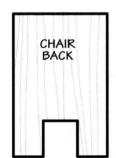

1.   You will want to make the back and legs of the chair from one piece of 1 x 8 pine; the legs measure 1-1/2-inches wide and 4-inches tall. Measure, draw, and cutout the legs. Now is a good time to suggest your child consider the appearance: Would she like to add initials, or a cutout design, or slats? What about adding knobs or a curve?

2. Make the seat and front legs from one piece of 1 x 8, cut in half widthwise. Trace around the back legs to make the front legs match and cut out. The other half of the 1 x 8 works nicely for the seat. Now fit the sawed edges together, and nail the seat to the front legs.

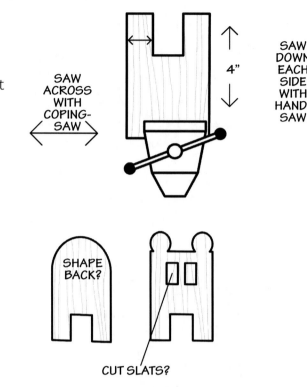

SAW ACROSS WITH COPING-SAW

SAW DOWN EACH SIDE WITH HAND-SAW

4"

ABC

♡

CARVE INITIALS OR DESIGNS?

SHAPE BACK?

CUT SLATS?

3. Draw a line half way down the chair back where it will meet the assembled seat and front legs. Match up the front and back legs to make sure they're even and the chair will not wobble. Then turn the front around again. Start nails just below the halfway line.

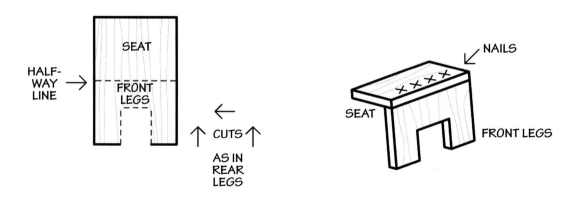

HALF-WAY LINE

SEAT

FRONT LEGS

CUTS

AS IN REAR LEGS

NAILS

SEAT

FRONT LEGS

(Hammer in only two nails to start, check for wobble, realign as needed, and complete nailing.)

4. Leg braces are cut from the last piece of 1 x 8. Trace the chair

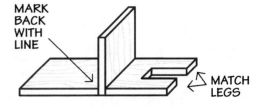

MARK BACK WITH LINE

MATCH LEGS

on the wood, divide that half in half lengthwise, cut, plane edges, and

START NAILS BELOW LINE

nail with 2 nails in each end. The leg braces are essential as they stabilize the chair. Place chair on one half of the 1 x 8,

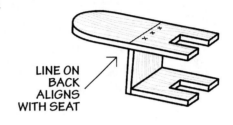

LINE ON BACK ALIGNS WITH SEAT

and trace a line around the inside between the legs. Bisect marked pieces for braces Aand B) After smoothing sawed edges, start nails, center across legs, and hammer in.)

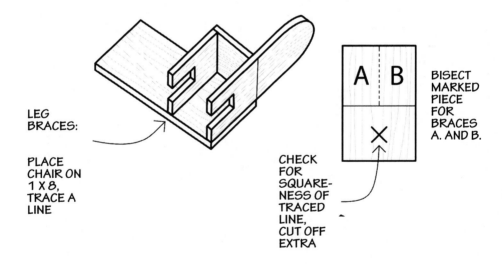

LEG BRACES:

PLACE CHAIR ON 1 X 8, TRACE A LINE

CHECK FOR SQUARENESS OF TRACED LINE, CUT OFF EXTRA

A	B

BISECT MARKED PIECE FOR BRACES A. AND B.

Comments: Children enjoy making things that are the "real deal" as well as whimsical, creative toys.

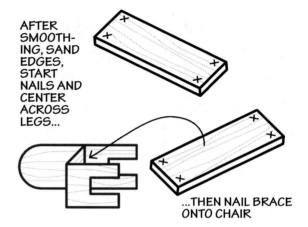

AFTER SMOOTH-ING, SAND EDGES, START NAILS AND CENTER ACROSS LEGS...

...THEN NAIL BRACE ONTO CHAIR

Bird House

Skill level: Intermediate

Time: 1-2 hours

Materials:

- 6 16-inch lengths of 1 x 8 pine
- 6d 2-inch finish nails
- 1/4-inch dowel or a small carvable piece of wood for perch
- thin scrap of wood about 2-inches long

Tools:

- Hammer
- Handsaw
- Coping saw
- Pencil
- Drill and 3/8-inch bit
- Try square
- 1-foot ruler
- Four-way combination rasp

Description – Here is one of those classic, satisfying projects most children adore. The birdhouse has a long, useful life and gives pleasure to all concerned, including the birds that take up residence within. It remains visible (hanging from a tree branch), and is fun to watch as birds go back and forth feathering their nest with twigs and other found materials, and then there's the pleasure of seeing the fledglings emerge for their first flight lessons.

Steps:

1. Start by making the front and back of the birdhouse. As these are identical pieces, it's best to trace the completed front on a second piece of pine, and cut out. Place them together in a vise

and smooth the edges
until they match.

2.   To cut the bird-
house door, draw or trace
the desired size hole in
the center of the front,
drill the hole inside the

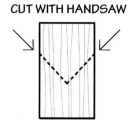

CUT WITH HANDSAW

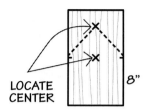

LOCATE
CENTER

8"

perimeter, disassemble and reassemble the coping saw so blade is
in the hole and cut out the circle.

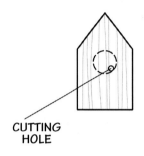

CUTTING
HOLE

SAW IN PLACE
FOR CUTTING

*Note: many birds are
fussy about their door
size. If you want to
attract a special bird,
best do some research
first to determine the
proper hole-size and
placement of the house.

Small children will be just as delighted with a starling, a less particular bird, but if you want to attract wrens or bluebirds, for example, you may want to guide your child accordingly.

3.   For the two sides, cut a 16-inch 1 x 8 in
half.

CUT IN HALF
WITH HANDSAW

4.   With the four sides completed, it's time to
assemble the birdhouse. Start the nails in front
and back 3/8-inch from edge. Align and nail one side to the front,
and then align and nail to the back.

START THE NAILS IN
FRONT AND BACK

EACH
SIDE IS
NAILED
TO THE
FRONT...

THEN THE BACK
IS ALIGNED
AND
NAILED
ON

5.   Like airplanes, birds need to land before they can go into the hole (or hanger).   To accommodate, drill a perch hole an inch or so below the door. and insert and glue a 2- to 3-inch long dowel.

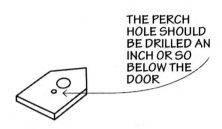

THE PERCH HOLE SHOULD BE DRILLED AN INCH OR SO BELOW THE DOOR

6.   The roof and floor are made of the same size boards. Kids can choose which they want to make first. Place the birdhouse on a piece of 1 x 8 pine and trace around the edges to cut the floor. Then nail on the floor from the bottom. For a pitched roof, start the nails at the apex, and lap the second piece over the first.

7.   You may want to hinge the second roof piece for easy clean-

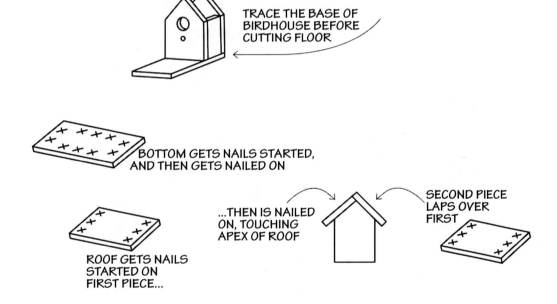

TRACE THE BASE OF BIRDHOUSE BEFORE CUTTING FLOOR

BOTTOM GETS NAILS STARTED, AND THEN GETS NAILED ON

...THEN IS NAILED ON, TOUCHING APEX OF ROOF

ROOF GETS NAILS STARTED ON FIRST PIECE...

SECOND PIECE LAPS OVER FIRST

ing between nesting seasons. (By the way, some birds like a clean apartment when they return from Disney World. Others do not like their nests disturbed. You will want to check to make sure.)

8.   Install perch, smooth edges, and paint a subtle color. Birds

don't like bright colors, but unfortunately kids do. Better decide who needs to be happier here, kids or birds.

Comments

This is a basic, no frills birdhouse, not designed for fussy, esoteric birds, but garden variety ones, delightful for children to watch. This little house structure lends itself to other adventures in wood, as well, such as a miniature doghouse for a stuffed toy, or with a square door cut in, a garage for a Ferrari, or a barn for toy horses, or whatever else comes to mind. The beauty of working with children is that ideas spring to mind quite easily.

Car

Ability Level: Intermediate – Advanced

Time: 2 to 3 hours

Materials:

- Two to three lengths of 1 x 8 pine

Tools:

- Coping saw
- 6d 2-inch finish nails
- Handsaw
- Vise
- Hammer
- 4-way combination rasp
- Block plane
- Hand drill with 3/8-inch bit
- Pencil

Description: The simplest and easiest cars to make are racecars or open-roofed sports cars or convertibles. Sedans, police cars, or buses that have windows and other details are harder, but all are doable, and all appeal to the avid woodworker who likes to take on new challenges.

Steps:

1. Start work on the side of the vehicle first. You can cut both sides of a racecar from one length of wood. After finding the centerline of the board length (see tricks of the trade), sketch the desired shape of the side, using the entire half-length. Cut out with a coping saw, smooth edges, and trace, cut out, and smooth as

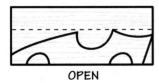

OPEN

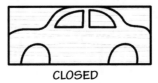

CLOSED

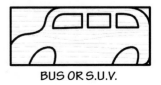

BUS OR S.U.V.

needed to make the second side identical to the first.

2.   Place one side on the edge of another piece of wood and let your child or student decide how wide she wants the vehicle. Then, mark a rectangle for the floor pan which will go between the two sides, and cut it with a handsaw. Plane the sawed edge and attach each side of the car to the floor pan.

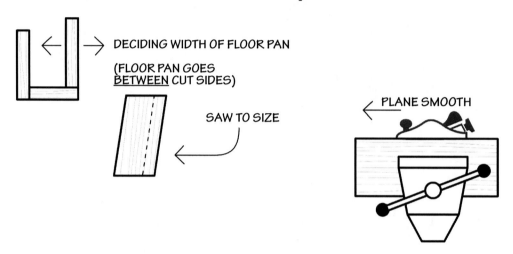

DECIDING WIDTH OF FLOOR PAN

(FLOOR PAN GOES BETWEEN CUT SIDES)

SAW TO SIZE

PLANE SMOOTH

3.   The hood and trunk lid will be the same width as the floor pan. Mark a strip of wood the same width as the floor pan, then cut hood and trunk lid to length with handsaw, plane carefully (don't let these pieces get too narrow or fitting will be hard), and nail down only one end (using 1 1/2-inch finish nails) if opening and closing is desired.

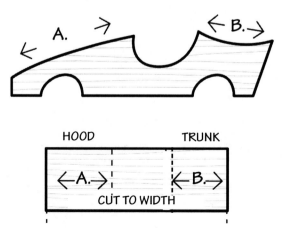

A.   B.

HOOD   TRUNK

A.   B.

CUT TO WIDTH

Take your time! Position the hood and trunk pieces carefully. Make sure the nail is positioned correctly to hit the edge of the side piece. It must remain straight throughout the nailing. The best approach is to drive the nail halfway

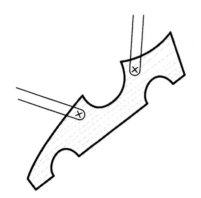

in, test the piece for opening and closing before completing the nailing. Then do the other side and check as you go, reposition as needed. The wood is liable to crack at this point if one nails incorrectly, a fixable but somewhat discouraging possibility.

4. If your child wants a roof, it should be carefully fitted, nailed or glued in.

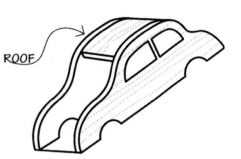

ROOF

5. Wheels need to fit in wheel openings. Best to find a round object to trace. Jar covers, and tin cans work. The wheel size will be around 2-inches in diameter. Trace four of them, cut out with coping saw, smooth and attach. (Here is where those small scraps and cuttings can be useful — saving a box of small pieces of wood is always a good idea.)

6. Seats, made from blocks of wood with little backrests, may also come right from your scrap box. Sometimes a steering wheel or a windshield, cut from Plexiglas scrap, lends a touch of realism. Use a coping saw to cut the Plexiglas, and cut very slowly and carefully because the Plexiglas is brittle and breaks easily. Drilling holes to attach the Plexiglas requires equal care, so take it easy. Everyone seems to have to break one or two pieces of Plexi, so take heart and try again. Perhaps it's a woodworker's rite of passage!

Comments: Note you and your child will encounter several projects with two identical sides – the box, the robot, the desk, and others in this book. These are challenging projects that require time, skill, and patience for young woodworkers, but they will love the results.

Desk

Ability level: Intermediate-Advanced

Time: 2 to 3 hours

Materials:

- Ten to eleven lengths of 16-inch 1 x 8 pieces
- 1 Pair 1/2-inch butt hinges and screws

Tools:

- Handsaw
- Hammer
- 6d 2-inch finish nails
- Pencil and ruler
- Block plane
- Four-way Combination rasp
- Vise
- Half-inch chisel

Description: A small child can sit at this twenty-inch-high desk with a pillow on the chair. Kids love the desk, and it can make a great present for a sibling or stuffed animal "student." According to the kids in my class, this project is definitely worth the effort.

Steps:

1.   You will work on the sides first. These are sloping pieces cut from two 1 x 8's measured 3 1/2-inches in from the top left side and 2 1/2-inches from the bottom right. Save the cut scraps to use for cleats. Smooth the sawed pieces and match them up by placing together in a vise and block-planing the cut edges to

CUTTING SIDES

3 1/2"

2 1/2"

CUT ONE, THEN TRACE FOR #2

make sure they are identical.

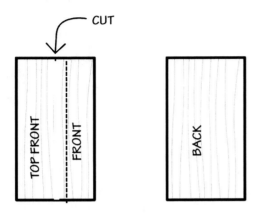

CUT

TOP FRONT

FRONT

BACK

2.   Next, cut the front, back, and flat top edge from equal pieces of 1 x 8's. The front comes from a 2 1/2-inch strip cut lengthwise from one 16-inch length; use the remainder for the top edge. After cutting, gently plane to smooth. The

desk back comes from the second piece of pine, and needs no cuts.

3.   Assemble the four sides now, attaching back and front to the two sides

4.   The bottom or floor of the desk comes from fitting two pieces of 1 x 8's inside and nailing them through from the outside all around the four sides . Sometimes a little planing on one or another of the floor pieces (lengthwise with the grain) will help these boards fit more snugly.

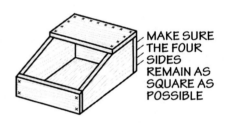

MAKE SURE THE FOUR SIDES REMAIN AS SQUARE AS POSSIBLE

5.   At this point, your child can either make the cover or the legs next. Either will work, but here we'll tackle the legs. The feet come from a piece of 1 x 8 bisected lengthwise with a hand saw. Round the two corners (this looks much better and lessens the

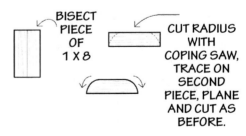

BISECT PIECE OF 1 X 8

CUT RADIUS WITH COPING SAW, TRACE ON SECOND PIECE, PLANE AND CUT AS BEFORE.

chance of stubbed toes later on) with a coping saw. Then plane the edges of all cut surfaces with the four-way combination rasp. The effect is quite satisfying and gives the desk a more finished look.

6. Attach a foot to one end of each of the legs with five nails, clinched inside , and attach the legs to the desk with six more nails), and clinch. When nailing the legs, make sure the first one is straight, then match the second, making the desk secure and stable. You do this by attaching with one nail, first, and checking for rocking before you complete the nailing.

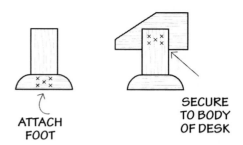

ATTACH FOOT

SECURE TO BODY OF DESK

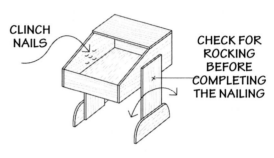

CLINCH NAILS

CHECK FOR ROCKING BEFORE COMPLETING THE NAILING

7. For the cover, make the basic platform (The first project in this book.) Use the scraps you

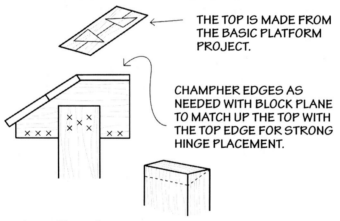

THE TOP IS MADE FROM THE BASIC PLATFORM PROJECT.

CHAMPHER EDGES AS NEEDED WITH BLOCK PLANE TO MATCH UP THE TOP WITH THE TOP EDGE FOR STRONG HINGE PLACEMENT.

saved after cutting the sides (see step 1) for the cleats. The top edges get champhered (planed to fit the top edge of the desk) to make the hinges easier to install, and stronger.

8. Now install the hinges and the desk is complete.

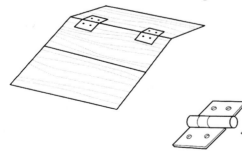

WITH THE FLAT SIDE OF THE HINGE FACING DOWN, COUNTERSINK OF HOLES UP, CENTER HINGES ACROSS THE TOP EDGE, MARK THE SCREW LOCATIONS ON THE COVER, ATTACH HINGES, THEN PLACE ON DESK, ALIGN AS NEEDED, MARK, AND START ONE SCREW IN EACH HINGE. NOW YOU WILL WANT TO TEST THE COVER BEFORE ADDING THE SECOND SCREW IN CASE YOU NEED TO REPOSITION THE HINGES.

9. For a further refinement to the finished desk, some kids like to add pencil traps. If so, sketch one out at the top edge, and carve with the chisel. Your child or students can also add letters or designs to the back face – easily done by tipping the desk on its front and carving

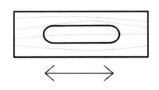

DRAW OUT AND CARVE A PENCIL TRAY

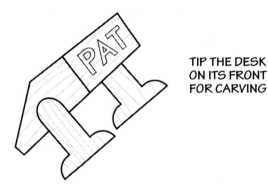

TIP THE DESK ON ITS FRONT FOR CARVING

Comments:

This is a time-consuming project demanding lots of work and the full array of skills your child has learned so far, which is why I call the desk "intermediate to advanced." It requires energy and commitment, as well as ability and strength. However, the desk remains one of the most popular projects for students who have the staying power and skills. The result is immensely rewarding.

Robot

Ability Level: Intermediate – Advanced

Time: 1 to 2-plus hours

Materials needed:

- Ten to twelve lengths of 1 x 8 pine
- 6d 2" finish nails

Tools:

- Vise
- 3/8-inch chisel
- Coping saw
- C clamp
- Pencil
- Handsaw
- Four-way combination rasp
- Hammer

Description: This is a large project. It takes a lot of time to make a robot due to the amount of cutting and assembling, but the results are quite wonderful and a real triumph for a child. When done it may well be as tall as the builder. This thrills kids.

Steps:

1. We work on the main body first. Pick four pieces of 1 x 8 pine as close to the same length as possible to allow for the best fit. On two pieces, mark and start 5 nails on each longitudinal edge, then assemble – it will look like a chimney when done.

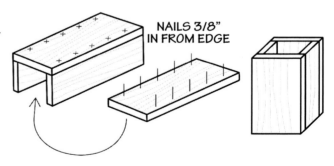

NAILS 3/8"
IN FROM EDGE

ALWAYS REMEMBER TO START NAILS FIRST:
SO MUCH EASIER!

2. Trace the top "shoulders" on another piece of 1 x 8, cut out with the handsaw, and attach to the top of the body with ten nails.

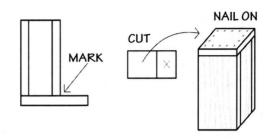

3. You will make the head from another piece of 1 x 8, cut into four equal pieces, and assembled like the box. Now trace around the outside of this box a square for the robot's face on another piece of 1 x 8 (clear pine if possible), and cut out. Sketch in the facial features and carve them out with your chisel. Nail the face on one side of the head. It will not be quite wide enough so for an optimal appearance you will want to cut a narrow strip to finish the edge of the face. You may want to add a back to the head.

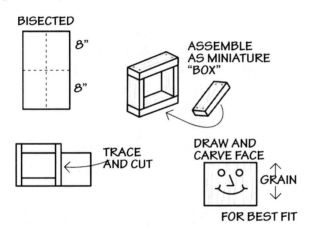

Some people find the hollow look a bit disturbing! If so, follow the same procedure as measuring, cutting, and nailing the face. Do support the head while doing this to prevent it from coming loose.

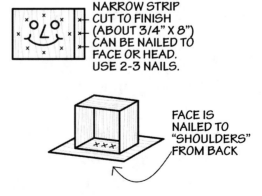

4. Nail face to shoulders inside the back of the box. Sometimes builders don't like the head being hollow. You can even hinge the back for easier

brain surgery — there are endless options out there, so take this opportunity to brainstorm and imagine.

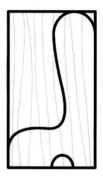

(ONE ROBOT GOT SPURS, ANOTHER GOT RAY GUNS ADDED TO FEET, ANY OTHER IDEAS?)

5.   Draw the robot's legs on another piece of 1 x 8 using the entire board. (Sometimes high heels are desired as line indicates.) Cut out with a coping saw and smooth the edges. Trace the second leg on another piece of 1 x 8 and cut; again smooth to create a nice finish.

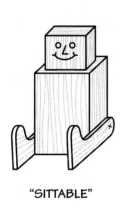

"SITTABLE"

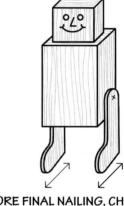

BEFORE FINAL NAILING, CHECK FOR LEG STABILITY AND ALIGNMENT

6.   It's up to your child to decide where to place the legs on the body. He can position them on each side so the robot stands straight. Does he want his robot to sit?   Sitting robots have trouble standing without falling because the legs are attached with only one nail, and thus have very little stability. Two nails in each leg prevent movement – now the robot stands nicely but it can't sit.

7.   Cut the hands and arms from leftover pieces. Decide on a design and shape, draw one, cut out, then smooth the edges and trace the second. Smooth the second and now decide the position and attach to the robot's body with just one nail each to make movement possible. Clinching them on the inside is not a bad idea

as frequent limb motion does loosen, and this will prevent the arms from falling off.

8. Feel free to accessorize: add soda cans, flags, ray guns, anything else that strikes your imagination, to the hands. *Optional*: Sometimes kids want the robot to have a bottom, which they can make the same size as the shoulders. Sometimes they like hinging the shoulder piece so they can put things inside the robot's body; simply hinge instead of nailing.

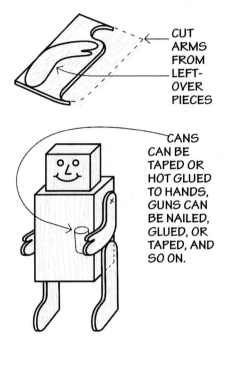

CUT ARMS FROM LEFT-OVER PIECES

CANS CAN BE TAPED OR HOT GLUED TO HANDS, GUNS CAN BE NAILED, GLUED, OR TAPED, AND SO ON.

Comments: This project is quite labor intensive and when a child succeeds in finishing it, the size as well as the accomplishment is cause to celebrate! Your child has done something major. It shows in all respects. Follow that up with a nice paint job — and wow, the robot springs to life!

Castle

Ability level: Intermediate - Advanced

Time: Probably 2 hours minimum

Materials Needed:

- Several 16-inch lengths of 1 x 8 pine
- 6d 2-inch finish nails
- 1 pair of 1-inch butt hinges and screws
- More or less of above material depending on complexity of castle chosen

Tools:

- Vise
- Hammer
- Handsaw
- Block plane
- Coping saw
- Four-Way combination rasp
- Appropriate screwdrivers for hinge screws
- (Chisel and C clamps)

Description: Let's start this project with the basic platform. Then add towers — up to four at the corners, and more inside; crenellated walls, a drawbridge, walkways behind the walls for soldier to stand in, dungeons for the bad guys, and a platform in the tower for Cinderella or Rapunzel. The castle can be quite simple or complex. The possibilities are endless and kids can give their imaginations full play here, especially as by this time they will feel comfortable and confident with the tools. By now, if your child has done many of the projects in this book, woodworking will have become part of their vocabulary of skills and creative expression.

Tower Construction:

1.   Bisect two pieces of 1 x 8 pine lengthwise to make a tower. Plane each pair together to make them the same and silky smooth.

2.   Mark crenellations: Make straight cuts with hand saw, cut across the bottom of the first pair with a coping saw.

MARK CRENELLATIONS

#1

#2

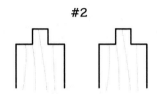

MAKE STRAIGHT CUTS WITH HANDSAW, CUT ACROSS BOTTOM (CROSS GRAIN) WITH COPING SAW

3.   Start nails and attach second pair between the first pair of sides. If you want a place for Rapunzel to stand, cut a small platform and nail it in about 1-inch below the top.

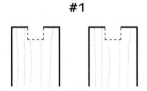

4.   If you want a dungeon, cut a "mouse door" in the fourth side with a coping saw (This is best done before you nail on the side.)

CUT A "MOUSE DOOR" IF YOU WANT TO MAKE A DUNGEON.

START NAILS, ATTACH PAIR #1 BETWEEN PAIR #2

5.   To nail the tower to the platform, trace on the bottom side the outline of where the tower will go; then start 6 nails 3/8-inch from edge. For more towers just repeat this process.

6   After towers are attached, the walls will be made from boards fitted between the towers. Crenellations add a grand touch of realism. Now cut out windows and doors if desired. You might want to consider a hinged drawbridge for authenticity and fun.

TRACE BOTTOM SIDE OF TOWER ON PLATFORM, THEN START NAILS.

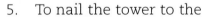

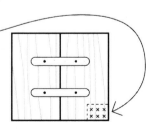

PIECE THAT IS CUT OUT
CAN BE HINGED AT BOTTOM SO THE
DRAWBRIDGE WILL WORK.

7.   Nail strips of wood in back of the walls right below the crenellations for the soldiers to have an easier time throwing down rocks and boiling oil. You can add machine guns or cannons to the crenellation for more fire power.

Comments: The castle can be as simple or elaborate as imagination, ability, and energy permit. The possibilities are endless and the process a lot of fun. It is important for parents to encourage creative departures, too. Take a look at castles in picture books or children's encyclopedias to get more ideas and to stretch this project's life a bit more. Your child might get excited about making flags to fly off the towers, or building a clay moat.

Mailbox

Ability Level: Advanced

Time: at least two hours

Materials Needed:

- Six to seven 16-inch lengths of 1 x 8 pine
- 6d 2-inch finish nails
- 1 pair 1-inch butt hinges (for front letter door)

Tools:

- Vise
- Handsaw
- Coping saw
- Hammer
- Bit brace
- Drill and 3/8-inch bit
- Block plane
- Four-way combination rasp

Description: Making a miniature mailbox has great fascination for children. A drop door at the top and a door at the bottom make it possible to put letters in and take them out (great for Valentine's Day, and other special occasions, as well as fantasy play.) This project has a longstanding record for challenging and rewarding all who make it.

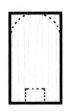

Steps:

1. First we will make the sides: to do this draw a radius top (like a real mailbox) on one board)

2. Draw legs at bottom (not too skinny and about 1 1/2 inches high. (Parents or older siblings or teachers may need to lend a hand with steps 1 and 2.)

3. Put the board in a vise and let your child cut the top with a

coping saw. Now, stand the board upside down in the vise, cut the legs with handsaw, up the sides and across with coping saw. (Always let your child do as much of the work as possible. By now, if you have had a chance to do many of the projects in this book, your child will be quite an accomplished woodworker.)

4. Trace the first side on another board, and repeat the drawing and cutting process on the second side.

5. Match both boards, place in the vise and smooth the tops, making them identical so the roof will fit well.

6. Mark the back—from the top of the cut at the legs to the lowest part of the curve, and draw a cut line. Now cut the back.

NAILS GO 3/8" IN FROM EDGE

"AND A ONE AND A TWO AND A THREE AND A FOUR."

AS LAWRENCE WELK USED TO SAY.

7. Match the sides again, mark four "x's" (or let your child do this) at points where your child will start the nails.

8. Start nailing together one side to the back so your child can complete the nailing, while you help with balancing the pieces on the worktable.

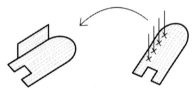

ADULT STARTS AND CHILD COMPLETES NAILING.

9. You can now position the second side against the back's other edge, get the nailing started, and then let your child complete.

MARK AND MEASURE THE FRONT

10. The front can now be marked and measured—it should be about 9-inches long. When cut, it will fit between the sides, the same height as the back so the legs look even.

11. Now it is time to choose. Do you want a door in the front so a letter can be easily removed? You will have to cut a rectangular hole in the front for removing letters, big enough for you child's

hand. First, draw it out, next, drill a hole in one corner, insert the coping saw blade, attach it to the saw, and cut out the hole. Smooth the edges of the hole with 4-way combination rasp.

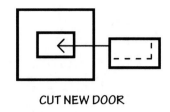

CUT NEW DOOR

12. Piece cut out of front will be too lumpy and has a hole cut out of corner so a new door piece will be needed. this is easily done from a scrap with a square corner. Trace using corner and two sides— kids love this: two "free" sides and two "need to cut" sides. Make the lines square and straight so it can be cut with a handsaw. Smooth door or hole to make door fit. Door can be hinged now or later— another choice. A carefully bent over nail makes a good handle.

13. Now you will want to start the nails for attaching the front. Place the mailbox on the worktable edge so it will not get broken. Fit in front and and nail one side. Start and nail other side. Once front is in place, back will be supported so nailing can be done on workbench. Put the mailbox on the workbench and attach the front of the box to the other side .

14. Now you will want to make the letter drop door. mark a piece of 1 x 8 to fit easily between each side. Cut piece will need to be cut again, with the grain, about 1 1/2" in from side.

PLACE THE MAILBOX ON THE WORKBENCH EDGE SO IT WILL NOT GET BROKEN

15. Plane sawed edges of each piece, nail the narrow piece at the top and back of front. the wider piece gets abent nail handle and one nail therough the sides at each lower edge so it will pivot forward to recieve the letter. It may take several tries to get pivot nails in the right place. Don't hammer them in all the way until you have made sure drop door passes the "pivot test."

16. Now it's time to give your mailbox a floor. Mark and cut a

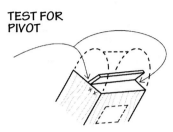

TEST FOR PIVOT

piece to that fits between and sides, front and back. Nail through outside to secure. Always remember to start nails first, position part to be nailed, then secure.

17.

The top (roof) is made by fitting another board between top and side arches circles, cut to fit and also cut lengthwise (wood grain should go long measurement side

MARK AND CUT A PIECE TO FIT BETWEEN THE SIDES

to side to facilitate planing the roof's roundness. (Don't forget to mark the letter door to receive the letters!) top boards are fitted as closely as possible together, nailed with 2 nails on each end.

18. "Roundness" of the roof is accomplished by clamping mail-box to workbench so top hangs over, Plaing can be done without hitting bench. Keep planing until the top looks like the real thing—

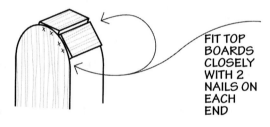

FIT TOP BOARDS CLOSELY WITH 2 NAILS ON EACH END

lots of work kids are delighted with the results

Comments: Congratulations on finishing your mailbox! The skill level for this project is quite advanced and carrying through requires much commitment, patience, and energy. Successful completion is hard won! Yet, the steps along the way are each doable and as with many things in life, the winner is the one who keeps going. It might take several woodworking sessions over a few days, but if you love working with wood, that's no hardship!

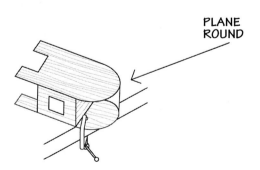

PLANE ROUND

PAINT AND FINISHES

Throughout *It Wood be Fun* I have suggested various ways to hone and finish projects by carving, making cutouts, add-ons, and painting. Perhaps most transforming of all is that bright fresh coat of paint. What is more satisfying than a simple all-red sailboat, for example, a blue chair, or a bookshelf with a scene or a name painted on the back?

Water-based poster paints work best for projects at this level because they are easy to mix, nontoxic, and washable. Of course it's always a good idea to wear a smock; most children enjoy putting on a big brother or sister's t-shirt or a smock for the task at hand. It makes them feel like real workers doing something that matters.

Water-based acrylics, more permanent and more likely to stain, are another option. Art stores carry them, and although not cheap, the basic colors will suffice and can be mixed on the job. That's another attribute of painting woodworking projects: children learn a lot about colors and gain dexterity handling a brush (three-quarters-of-an-inch width for brushes is the best).

 Clear finishes can be a simple coat of shellac, or a coat of water-based varnish, all applied after painting, if desired. Shellac offers protection and permanence. Use denatured alcohol for cleanup of shellac, and a cheap one-inch bristle brush for application.

For older, more experienced children, I recommend water-based latex paint available at house paint and hardware stores. It has a durable, hard finish and great coverage, but it comes with caveats; among them the facts that it stains badly, is harder to apply, cannot easily be mixed to create different colors at home, and has unpleasant but not unhealthy fumes. Use nylon brushes as chemicals will damage other bristle types.

Staining with poster paint or acrylic is another option. This allows the wood grain to show through. To do this apply a very thin coat of paint (with quite a bit of water added), and smooth on with a rag. Latex paint does not work for this method; much better to buy a stain and follow the instructions on the can. Stains, available from, hardware and paint stores, come in the appropriate consistency.

Painting and shellacking are important aspects of creating a finished project. Children need to know this so they take their job seriously. Holidays, as we call gaps in the paint, are unacceptable. Be reassured it takes no special talent to completely paint something, just patience and caring. You can point this out in a cheerful, upbeat way by saying something like, "Let's think expert, professionals hate holidays on their projects." Parents, older siblings, and teachers can help children set their sights higher to "be the best they can be." This, after all, is what learning any art or craft is all about.

EPILOGUE

The projects in this book offer endless opportunities for creative play, intellectual growth, and skill building. Here's a chance for adults to model behavior, to guide a child gently through tasks, and to engage in an ongoing one-on-one conversation. What kid would not want to use real tools to make real things that have long lives as toys, furniture, or objects of whimsy, art, and cheer?

I like to think of these projects influencing children for life. I have seen this happen! Just as a child will have her hammer and screwdriver long into adulthood, so too will the skills learned from woodworking endure. The subliminal and in many cases quite obvious lessons (but never call them that in front of the kids) involve measuring, math, eye-hand coordination; and quite possibly reading, writing, storytelling, and research. Your child will develop a keen eye for design, quite possibly a sense of organization (or at least its value!), and learn how to handle paint and mix colors. As with any art, craft, intellectual endeavor, or sport, all the projects from the platform to the mailbox demand patience, perseverance, imagination, and follow-through.

They also teach pride. Children who are shy, lacking in self-confidence, or more thoughtful (sometimes called dreamy in the classroom) will find themselves in an arena low in stress, competition, and social pressures. At the workbench we like to see solid workmanlike skills (drive a straight nail, saw a clean line, plane and smooth one piece to match another) and a reasonable helping of perfectionism. This book teaches basic rules for life: never accept less than your best, and always treat tools and other people with respect and care.

I hope you and your child (younger sibling, or student) enjoy making some or all of the projects in this book. If your kid finishes the mailbox and wants to know "What next?" I am convinced you and he will be able to design your own projects or look through woodworking magazines for inspiration and guidance. Should woodworking turn into a serious long-term pursuit; then it may be time to turn to a friendly carpenter or woodworking teacher for mentoring, ideas, sketches, and dialogue.

In the meantime, no need to look further ahead than the next project: Enjoy the moment and the innate creative capacity of children to learn, to lead the way, and to teach grownups so much more than we can ever teach them.

—M. B.-S.

GLOSSARY

Coming-out party   Nail that starts crooked and pokes out through the side of a project.

Cross the vise trick   Procedure for starting a nail in the side of a cylindrical object by placing it (on a slant) across a partially opened vise so it won't roll.

Heirloom quality   Project so wonderful and well-made it will have value to your child and maybe even your grandchildren.

Holiday   Housepainter's term for a missed place in the paint job.

Kerf   Pathway a saw makes going through a board.

Money-back guarantee   A problem that comes up in a project that is not the child's fault; I fix it; the child gets bailed out, the project saved.

Rubber nail   Nail that gets bent over while being hammered.